Ancillary Relief: A Guide to the New Rules

Ancillary Relief: A Guide to the New Rules

Nicholas Mostyn QC

John Nicholson, MA (Oxon), Solicitor, Barrister

Butterworths
London Edinburgh and Dublin
2000

United Kingdom	Butterworths, a Division of Reed Elsevier (UK) Ltd, Halsbury House, 35 Chancery Lane, LONDON WC2A 1EL and 4 Hill Street, EDINBURGH EH2 3JZ
Australia	Butterworths, a Division of Reed International Books Australia Pty Ltd, CHATSWOOD, New South Wales
Canada	Butterworths Canada Ltd, MARKHAM, Ontario
Hong Kong	Butterworths Asia (Hong Kong), HONG KONG
India	Butterworths India, NEW DELHI
Ireland	Butterworth (Ireland) Ltd, DUBLIN
Malaysia	Malayan Law Journal Sdn Bhd, KUALA LUMPUR
New Zealand	Butterworths of New Zealand Ltd, WELLINGTON
Singapore	Butterworths Asia, SINGAPORE
South Africa	Butterworths Publishers (Pty) Ltd, DURBAN
USA	Lexis Law Publishing, CHARLOTTESVILLE, Virginia

ISBN: 040693178X

Printed by Bookcraft (Bath) Limited, Midsomer Norton, Avon

Visit Butterworths LEXIS *direct* at: http://www.butterworths.com

Preface

This completely new book, aimed at all family law practitioners whose practice includes ancillary relief work, is a comprehensive guide to The Family Proceedings (Amendment No 2) Rules, 1999 ('The Amended Rules'). The Amended Rules will alter completely the form of application for, and the conduct of, ancillary relief applications in England and Wales, by replacing the old system with a modified version of the so-called 'Pilot Scheme', which was introduced in selected Courts back in October 1996. The Amended Rules come into force on 5 June, 2000. It is therefore vital that all practitioners are up-to-speed by then with the radical departure from current practice which they represent. Even those practitioners who have been working with the Pilot Scheme Rules since their inception must be aware that The Amended Rules make some very significant changes to the Pilot Scheme system, which they will ignore at their peril.

This book takes the reader step-by-step through The Amended Rules. It explains how each stage in the process operates and what needs to be done within which time limits. It offers a practical insight into how to tackle First Appointments, Financial Dispute Resolution Appointments and the all-important Form E. It comes complete with copies of the Rules themselves, and of all the forms annexed to the Rules which form part of the new procedure.

Both the authors are Ancillary Relief specialists, who have worked with the Pilot Scheme from its inception. Nicholas Mostyn, QC is a leading family law barrister and a Deputy High Court Judge of the Family Division. He is a member of the Lord Chancellor's Ancillary Relief Advisory Group, and speaks extensively on all aspects of Ancillary Relief work. He is in addition an expert on the Child Support Acts and his book *Child's Pay* is recognised as the leading textbook in that field. John Nicholson is a Solicitor in the Family Law Department at Manches Solicitors in London. Ancillary Relief work forms the bulk of his practice. He has written extensively in legal publications, and his a layman's guide to divorce *No, You Don't Get Half* is in preparation for publication later this year. He is also an occasional lecturer.

Contents

CHAPTER 1 – INTRODUCTION AND BACKGROUND

Introduction

1.01   On 5 June 2000, if you are a lawyer practising Ancillary Relief in England and Wales, the bottom is going to drop out of your world. The fear of falling will be less acute in those who operate principally in the so-called 'Pilot Scheme' Courts, and many practitioners will have had at least some limited experience of the Pilot Scheme when working away from their home patch. However, the 1999 amendments make some radical changes to the Pilot Scheme, which was itself a complete departure from the old-style Ancillary Relief procedure under the Family Proceedings Rules 1991 (FPR 1991), with which most of us grew up. To some extent, as at 5 June, we are all back to square one.

Background

1.02   In September 1991 the Senior District Judge delivered a paper to the Bar Conference in which he revisited the guidelines offered by Booth J in *Evans*[1]. He suggested that the conduct of middle and small money cases was still out of hand and that costs were being wasted on excessive affidavit evidence, requests for discovery, expert evidence and lack of court control. He suggested that the parties should be confined to one affidavit each; that at an initial directions appointment there should be strict judicial control of discovery and expert evidence; and that the pre-trial review procedure should be revived.

1   [1990] 1 FLR 319.

1.03   In March 1992, at the Solicitors Family Law Association (SFLA) annual conference Booth J returned to the topic in an address entitled *'Life after Evans'*[1]. She endorsed the views of the Senior District Judge stating :
> 'This would require a directions appointment to take place at the outset of any ancillary relief application and for the court to define the issues and to take over control in relation to the evidence, the inquiries, the valuations and the timing of proceedings thereafter.'

1   (See [1992] Fam Law 178)

1.04   In that same month the Family Law Bar Association (FLBA) proposed detailed changes to the FPR 1991 along these lines for consideration by the Family Proceedings Rules Committee. Although supported by the majority, their late arrival led to the conclusion that they needed further consideration by the Lord Chancellor's Department (LCD). In fact the committee did not meet again before the pilot scheme commenced. At about the same time, and independently, Jane Simpson and Helen Ward of the SLFA devised a draft scheme to meet the concerns expressed by the profession and endorsing the concerns of Booth J: that draft scheme was therefore ready and available to form part of the discussion with the Judiciary and the Bar which followed.

1.05   In the absence of meetings of the Family Proceedings Rules Committee, Thorpe LJ convened an *ad hoc* group to consider the matter. It became known as the Ancillary Relief Working Party. It first met in July 1992, and a draft rule was quickly agreed and drafted. It drew, to quite an extent, on the Australian model for court control of money cases, and in particular on its procedure of a pre-trial privileged 'conciliation conference' held before a Registrar. The rule drafted at that time was not really very different from the final Pilot Scheme. Subsequently, the group became nationalised by the LCD and became known as the Lord Chancellor's Advisory Group on Ancillary Relief (ARAG).

1.06   In June 1994 Lord Woolf began his process of consultation on civil justice procedural reform. This seemed to provide an impetus for acceptance of ARAG's proposals. By July 1995 the Lord Chancellor was able to signify his agreement to the proposals, but he stipulated that they must be tested by a pilot scheme. That pilot began, as we have said, in October 1996.

1.07   The scheme's implementation owes much to the ceaseless energy and creativity of Thorpe LJ, who would frequently burst into print when he perceived that enthusiasm was waning. Thus in *S v S* [1] decided on 29 July 1993, he said:
> 'This case provides an illustration of the harm that can be done within the system provided by the current Family Proceedings Rules for the determination of financial disputes. That system is essentially permissive: the court only controls when its powers are invoked. Shortcomings have been recognised by the Family Division Judges and district judges as well as the specialist bar and specialist solicitors. The case for change to greater control by the court, including court controlled mediation, has recently been advocated by a Principal Registry working party. Illustrations such as this strengthen the case for change.'

1   [1995] 1 FCR 149 at 159A.

1.08   In July 1994 he wrote the article in Family Law entitled 'Ancillary Relief in the Role of Cinderella' [1], explaining the scheme and ending with the words:
> 'I am convinced that the scheme promises to make better use of existing judicial resources at an administrative cost which will be shown as small compared to the gain achieved'.

1   [1994] Fam Law 362.

1.09   Similarly in *F v F* [2] decided on 24 October 1994 he said:
> 'The group first met in July 1992 and relatively swiftly thereafter detailed proposed amendment to the rules drafted by the FLBA were accepted by all members of the working party. Progress since has been frustratingly slow and the prospect of amendment to the current rules remains an uncertain one'

1   [1995] 2 FLR 45 at 69.

1.10   It must have given him great pleasure to have stated in his judgment in *Dart v Dart* [1]:
> 'Costs of this magnitude are almost unknown in this jurisdiction [*the wife's were £1,336,400, the husband's £801,669*]. They are a condemnation of our present procedures. On 1 October next new procedures are to be put on trial. These new procedures are designed to ensure amongst other objectives that the court and not the parties controls the escalation of costs.'

1   [1996] 2 FLR 286.

1.11   Experiences from many courts were assimilated by ARAG in devising the Rule. The group was particularly influenced by the Bristol procedure.

1.12 KPMG were brought in to analyse the Pilot Scheme and to report on its effectiveness in controlling costs and speeding up the resolution of ancillary relief cases. Despite a lengthy gestation period, their report, when it arrived, was widely regarded as unimpressive. In an interview given just before his retirement[1], Sir Stephen Brown, then President of the Family Division, summed up the feelings of many who read it when he said: *'Like many people who worked with the pilot scheme I was disappointed by the KPMG report, but I have to say that it has not been universally accepted as either helpful or reliable'*. He continued: *'The reports which I have from District Judges across the country are very much more encouraging than anything between its covers'*. It may be that the enthusiasm of those who were working with it played a large part in persuading the Lord Chancellor that, despite a downbeat report, the 'Pilot' should be rolled out, with appropriate amendments, nationwide.

1 The SFLA Review, December, 1999.

1.13 During the currency of the Pilot Scheme, ARAG continued to work hard, taking into consideration the countless brickbats and bouquets which were coming in from the 'guinea pig' practitioners, clients and Courts. This culminated in the current amendment to the FPR 1991, which replace those Rules from Section 2.52 to Section 2.68 inclusive.

The new rules: the overriding objective

1.14 Before commencing with the substantive amendments, Rule 2.51A provides definitions of 'applicant' and 'respondent', and provides for the use of 'FDR appointment' to stand for 'Financial Dispute Resolution appointment', of which more later. Then, in Rule 2.51B (1), it is stated 'The ancillary relief rules are a procedural code with the overriding objective of enabling the court to deal with cases justly'. The idea of an overriding objective, which is in terms categorised, was borrowed from the Civil Procedure Rules.

1.15 At sub paragraph (2), the notion of 'dealing with a case justly' is clarified to include a number of objectives, as follows.

'Ensuring that the parties are on an equal footing' [(2)(a)]

1.16 Although the idea of equality of arms will permeate all aspects of the new procedure, it is in the field of presentation of evidence that its impact will be most obvious. A fundamental tenet of the Amended Rules is that each party should present their evidence as far as possible in the same format. Under the 1991 Rules, where evidence is by narrative affidavit, much impact, inevitably, was made by the quality of the narrative. Although it is generally recognised that few judges are overly impressed by florid language and the minutely detailed reporting of the early months of a twenty year marriage, considerable resources can be allocated to the putting of the best possible gloss on a party's behaviour during a marriage. The belief is that, even in the majority of cases where 'conduct' for the strict purposes of Section 25 of the Matrimonial Causes Act 1973 is not in issue, a tribunal may be influenced at the margin by the skilfully sympathetic portrayal of a case. Clearly, if one party can afford the best draftsmen, and the other cannot, unfairness can creep in.

1.17 The Amended Rules replace the traditional narrative affidavit with a standard financial disclosure form, Form E, which is designed for the bland recital of financial facts. The form leaves little scope for the aspiring writer. It also makes it very clear to the reader when questions have been evaded, ignored, or answered economically: such flaws are much harder to conceal without the thick gloss paint of narrative. This in turn makes the drafting of questionnaires easier, and therefore cheaper.

'saving expense'[(2)(b)]

1.18   A number of practitioners have complained that this is, in fact, the Lord Chancellor's single 'overriding objective'. If so, he seems to have failed to achieve it, at least so far as experience of the Pilot Scheme has tended to show. Certainly the KPMG report, in one of the few of its findings which did not attract criticism, considered that the scheme appeared to be cost neutral when compared with the procedure under the FPR 1991. Indeed, many solicitors have concluded that the Pilot Scheme tends to 'front load' costs. Similar criticisms have been made of the new procedures under the CPR. However, the encouragement under the Amended Rules to use the First Appointment as an FDR where possible may alter that position. In any event, anecdotal evidence, if not the KPMG report, suggests that, particularly as a result of the introduction of Financial Dispute Resolution appointments, more cases settle before expensive preparations have to be made for a final hearing.

'dealing with the case in ways which are proportionate: to the amount of money involved; to the importance of the case; to the complexity of the issues; and to the financial position of each party'[(2)(c)(i)-(iv)]

1.19   The golden rule here appears to be to treat each case very specifically on its own merits, and to tailor the work which one does on it very specifically to its own set of facts. If judges are being astute, they will pick up (and presumably criticise in costs orders) practitioners who have run up costs unnecessarily by using 'standard' questionnaires and requests for documents. Practitioners who have been used to working on the principle of 'no piecemeal disclosure', and have therefore been inclined to ask as early as possible for everything they might possibly need, had better think again. Some critics have suggested that this is a recipe for future negligence actions, as solicitors ask for too little disclosure in a bid to avoid judicial criticism, and then miss something. Why should this be? In fact, modest disclosure of documents can concentrate the mind, and make it frankly more likely that the documents which are provided are analysed thoroughly. As the Amended Rules, unlike the Pilot Scheme, provide for significant documentary disclosure to be provided *ab initio*, the subsequent questionnaire is likely to be a more finely honed tool than was often possible under Rule 2.63. In any event, one can always return to the Court and ask for further disclosure (as was ever the case) if further legitimate queries arise.

1.20   What, though, do the Amended Rules mean when they refer to 'the importance of the case'? There are few practitioners whose practice principally comprises clients who think that their case is unimportant. If the importance of a case was measured by its legal complexity, or whether it might break new ground, then very few cases would fit the bill. Is it the money involved? Surely not. Many 'big money' cases are comparatively simple to resolve, precisely because there is plenty to go round. Indeed, disclosure may be much more limited, paradoxically, in a case where a husband has vast wealth, simply because his wife's reasonable needs can easily be met, than in a case with more modest assets, where there is a need to find and divide every last penny, and creative thinking is at a premium.

'ensuring that it is dealt with expeditiously and fairly' [(2)(d)]

1.21 Perhaps 'expeditiously *but* fairly' would more accurately have encapsulated this goal. One of the greatest triumphs of the Pilot Scheme has been the way that cases under its rules are progressed consistently, and not allowed to drift. The danger of expedition is that omissions may be overlooked and discounted, and precision sacrificed on the altar of speed. Pilot Scheme practitioners have not, in our experience, so far fallen at this potential hurdle, but everyone involved in the implementation of the Amended Rules must be vigilant to ensure that tight time limits are not permitted to become an excuse for cutting corners.

'allotting to it an appropriate share of the court's resources, while taking into account the need to allot resources to other cases' [(2)(e)]

1.22 This is likely to vary from judge to judge and from court to court. Does a case merit more than the standard hour for an FDR? Does the judge require additional reading time? Will he be able to send the parties and their advisors away after their appointment and invite them back into court an hour or two later after further negotiations? All these things are frequently appropriate and helpful, but not necessarily possible in practice. Our experience has been that many judges operating under the Pilot Scheme have been at pains to help cases to settle, often truncating lunch adjournments, or sitting late or early to accommodate those who are near agreement. It will be interesting to see whether this trend will continue nationally once the Amended Rules are rolled out. In any event, if you think that you are close to settling, always ask for more time.

What should we all be doing, and how?

1.23 Paragraphs (3) to (6) of Rule 2.51B state that not only must the court seek to give effect to the overriding objective when exercising power given to it by the ancillary relief rules[1], or when interpreting any rule[2], but also that the parties, too, are required to help the court to further the overriding objective[3].

1 Rule 2.51B (3)(*a*).
2 Rule 2.51B (3)(*b*).
3 Rule 2.51B (4).

1.24 The court is charged with furthering the overriding objective by actively managing cases[1] in the following ways[2]:

(a) *encouraging the parties to co-operate with each other in the conduct of proceedings*
Experience of the Pilot Scheme has taught us that judges take widely differing views of the form that this encouragement should take. Some content themselves with a mild warning at both the First Appointment and at the FDR that costs will escalate significantly between that hearing and the next. Others, with a more robust standpoint, will harangue everyone in the courtroom with a view of the profligate waste which is being perpetrated in the light of the limited resources available. Then again, there are some who say rather sadly at the close of an FDR that it really is a shame that the parties cannot get any closer than they are. To be fair, while it is easy to criticise judges for being feeble in their pronouncements; for there are cases under the Pilot Scheme which have reached the FDR stage, still one side's financial position is shrouded in mystery, and it is virtually

impossible to see where any consensus or compromise might be reached. At this point it may be possible for a judge to progress the case by:

(b)   *encouraging the parties to settle their disputes through meditation*
but this is more likely to be successful after a First Appointment where little or no further disclosure is needed, and where the parties are at least reasonably clear about what the areas of disagreement are. Wholly unsuccessful FDRs are frequently the result of not

(c)   *identifying the issues at an early date*
which is itself usually the result of woefully inadequate disclosure by one party (which often happens to the paying party). Anyone who has practised under the Pilot Scheme will have recollections of outrageously inadequate disclosure in Form E, with whole sections left blank, and totally inadequate replies. Businessmen will maintain that the value of their business assets is 'difficult to establish', without explaining why, or that their income from the business for this financial year and last is 'as yet unclear', with no corroboration from an accountant. This kind of behaviour simply wastes time, and makes it impossible to focus on any issue, save that the miscreant's financial affairs are no clearer than they were before the Form E was filed. Inevitably, the other party's questionnaire then has to be constructed partly as a means of establishing the detail which should have been provided in the Form E, and the drafter is forced to 'take a stab' at what further disclosure might be relevant. Such recalcitrance must not, we suggest, be tolerated. The judge may, at a First Appointment, fix a further directions appointment rather than an FDR[3]. Why should he not insist that the form is completed properly, with all the required documentation for which the Amended Rules make provision[4]? Once the issues have been identified, the court can then address them.

(d)   *regulating the extent of disclosure of documents and expert evidence so that they are proportionate to the issues in question*
The 'regulation' (or, as some critics prefer, the 'limiting') of disclosure under the Pilot Scheme has prompted some strenuous arguments. The most extreme of these has been the question of whether the Lord Chancellor's department has the right to formulate rules which place any limit on disclosure, or whether this should rather be achieved by primary legislation. Certainly, the Pilot Scheme was particularly draconian in permitting no disclosure, save Form E, between the issue of an application in Form A, and the direction relating to replies to questionnaire within the order made at the First Appointment. This inflexibility, it has been argued, hampered early settlement in some cases, because practitioners feared that even reasonable requests for documents made where there was goodwill on both sides could not be accommodated without falling foul of the Rules.
However, the Amended Rules have been drafted specifically to deal with this shortcoming, while still attempting to keep the lid on the quantum of disclosure at an early stage. The Form E must now be accompanied by a raft of prescribed documents (of which more later). These are intended to provide sufficient disclosure in the majority of cases to enable meaningful offers to be made, and to encourage, in as many cases as possible, the use of the First Appointment, in whole or in part, as an FDR. The court does not further the overriding objective merely by making directions. It should be

(e)   *helping the parties to settle the whole or part of the case*
This requires a different judicial approach at the beginning of ancillary relief cases from the one that most judges are accustomed to take. At the First Appointment under the Amended Rules, as in the Pilot Scheme, the judge will

have before him a Statement of the Apparent Issues provided by each party. Armed with these documents, he may then voice his opinion, or his concerns, directly to the parties (who must be present[5]). He will, of course be in a stronger position to do so if offers have already been made on the strength of the initial disclosure, and the First Appointment is being treated as an FDR. The wording of this rule also makes it clear that any progress is to be welcomed. If a division of capital can be agreed, while maintenance remains in dispute, at least the issues have been narrowed. Even so, practitioners should be wary of the fact that FDR appointments are wholly without prejudice. An agreement on one part of a settlement will not be binding on a party in the absence of an overall agreement, although its existence must be brought to the attention of a judge conducting a further FDR[6]. One of the court's duties is

(f)   *fixing timetables or otherwise controlling the progress of the case*

This, too is a departure from traditional practice. The court *must* move the case forward in any but the most exceptional circumstances, *usually* by fixing a further directions appointment or adjourning for out of court mediation[7]. He should not permit the parties or their advisors to allow the case to drift. To what extent it is realistic at present to expect the court to be

(g)   *making use of technology*

is as yet unclear. Will judges expect parties to use self help for the provision of, for example, company accounts, via the internet? Does the rule envisage an in-court computer system and access to 'virtual' trial bundles containing documents which have been scanned into the system. Maybe so, but at present such case management is extremely expensive and, as far as we are aware, only the High Court has the facilities to deal with it. The final part of the court's duty in actively managing cases consists of

(h)   *giving directions to ensure that the trial of a case proceeds quickly and efficiently*

and is presumably intended to fit with sub-paragraph (f), above. Again, it requires the judge to tailor the new system to fit the individual case. For example, progress has been made at an FDR, but no settlement has been agreed. Should the judge set the case down for a final hearing and warn the parties about the costs, but risk losing the momentum which has been built up in the run up to the FDR? Should he instead bring the parties back sooner for another FDR, and risk significant further costs if no further progress is made? Or how about a further directions appointment, if they are very close, or even a mention, if they have all but dotted the 'i's and crossed the 't's?

1   Rule 2.51B (5).
2   Rule 2.51B (6)(a)–(g).
3   Rule 2.61D(2)(d)(i).
4   Rule 2.61B(3)(a), (b).
5   Rule 2.61D(5).
6   Rule 2.61E(3), (4).
7   Rule 2.61D(2)(d).

1.25   How, though are we to ensure that the parties fulfil the requirement upon them to help the court to further the overriding objective? How can practitioners prevent those of their clients who have their own agenda from digging their heels in and being uncooperative? Presumably as we have always done, by issuing stiff warnings about the costs implications of that kind of behaviour. Now we can tell obstructive clients that under the amended Rules the courts will be more proactive, and are more likely than hitherto to make costs orders against parties who are dragging their heels. The judges will need to be decisive if the message is to come across, but the indications from both Pilot Scheme courts and others is that this decisiveness will be forthcoming.

CHAPTER 2– AN OVERVIEW OF THE NEW PROCEDURE

2.01   As of 5 June, 2000, all applications for ancillary relief in England and Wales will be made in the same way; a variation on the Pilot Scheme which has been in place since October 1996 in 29 'guinea pig' courts (including the Principal Registry) around the country.

2.02   The Amended Rules provide for a tripartite procedure before an eventual final hearing. This is designed to enable as many cases as possible to settle without going to a full final hearing. First, there is a period for initial disclosure after the issuing of an application for ancillary relief, in the run up to a mandatory directions appointment, the First Appointment. Secondly, there is the First Appointment itself which may, if the parties wish and/or the judge considers appropriate, be used as an attempt to settle the case with judicial assistance. Thirdly, there is further disclosure, followed by a kind of court-led mediation session, the Financial Dispute Resolution Appointment, or FDR. In normal circumstances, only if there is no settlement after all these stages have been completed, will there be a final hearing.

2.03   M11s and M13s will disappear, both being replaced by a single new form of application, the Form A[1]. From 5 June, 2000, anyone wishing to make an application for ancillary relief must file a notice of intention do so in Form A[2]. Once the application is issued, the relevant court will set a date for a First Appointment. This must be neither less than 12 weeks, nor more than 16 weeks after the date of the filing of the notice. Five weeks before the First Appointment the parties must exchange sworn statements of their financial circumstances in Form E, together with a number of prescribed documents. No less than 14 days before the First Appointment, they must file and serve a concise statement of the issues between them, a chronology, and Questionnaires, including requests for any further documents required, which must be related to the statement of issues. They may also decide whether or not they wish to use all or part of the First Appointment as an FDR.

1   Rules 7, 9(2), 9(4)(a) of the Family Proceedings (Amendment No 2) Rules 1999.
2   Or, rarely, Form B. See p 10, below.

2.04   At the First Appointment, the judge will give directions relating to replies to Questionnaire and matters such as valuations and other expert evidence. He will also give directions relating to the further disposition of the case including, unless exceptionally he decides that it is inappropriate, the fixing of a date for an FDR. He may, in exceptional circumstances, make an order for costs, although this is likely to be rare.

2.05   The FDR exists for the purpose of discussions and negotiation. It should be seen as a without prejudice meeting, at which the judge will see *all* the offers made in the case. These must be filed at least 7 days before the FDR. As a result, that judge may not take part in the case again, other than to conduct a further FDR. The judge may indicate what he sees as an appropriate level of settlement in the case, and the parties are required to use their best endeavours to reach agreement on the matters in issue before them. It goes without saying that both parties must be personally present at an FDR. If an acceptable settlement is brokered, the court may make a final order at the conclusion of the appointment. If no conclusion is reached, then the court will probably set the case down for trial, making attendant directions about the filing of evidence. It is open, though, to a judge, to list a further FDR, or further directions, if it seems very likely that there will be a settlement shortly.

The final hearing of a case has the same format as under the old Rules and the Pilot Scheme, but with some important differences with respect to the issue of costs in relation to *Calderbank* offers, with which we deal in detail below.

2.06　Finally, there are nine new forms within the procedure under the Amended Rules. Each is replicated in full in appendix A. The forms are as follows:

- Form A:　　Notice of [intention to proceed with] an application for Ancillary Relief;
- Form B:　　Notice of an application under Rule 2.45 (financial hardship);
- Form C:　　Notice of First Appointment;
- Form D:　　Notice of a Financial Dispute Resolution Appointment;
- Form E:　　Financial Statement;
- Form F:　　Notice of Allegation in Proceedings for Ancillary Relief;
- Form G:　　Notice of response re: First Appointment;
- Form H:　　Costs Estimate;
- Form I:　　Notice of Request for Periodical Payments Order at same rate as Order for Maintenance Pending Suit.

Chapter 3 – MAKING AN APPLICATION – FORM A

3.01　A notice of intention to proceed with an application for ancillary relief made in a petition or answer, or an application for ancillary relief, must be made in Form A. This must be filed either in the divorce county court in which the divorce proceedings are pending or, if the case is pending in the High Court, in the registry in which it is proceeding[1]. A Form A may be filed at any time after a petition has been issued. A template Form A may be found at p 70 in appendix A, below.

1　Rule 2.61A(1), (2).

Completing Form A

3.02　The template Form A which forms an annexure to the Amended Rules is a revision from the original used in the Pilot Scheme. The inclusion of 'check boxes' for the various orders for which a client may be applying was presumably considered more helpful than a blank space. However, a difficulty arises. The form does not make it clear that the Court still requires full information about property (including who owns it, whether or not it is mortgaged, and the Land Registry Title Number, if you have it). Furthermore, it provides neither for separate orders for the children, not for an order under the Pensions Act, 1995, if appropriate. These inclusions will, therefore, have to be made manually, a task which can produce an untidy and confusing final product with some of the less flexible on-screen forms.

3.03　Remember that, when you file the Form A, the court will list a First Appointment between 12 weeks and 14 weeks from the date of filing. Unless you obtain permission to the contrary from the court (most easily achieved by taking a consent application to the District Judge of the day or by *ex parte* application before the District Judge as a short time summons at the beginning of his or her list), your client must attend that appointment. Try to ensure that when you file you are armed with a list of unavailable dates during that period both for yourself and your client. Pilot Scheme practitioners have found that, by and large, the courts are helpful about avoiding clashes. It is also possible to move a First Appointment if the other party has an unavoidable clash of dates, for example a holiday which has already been booked, or an important business meeting which cannot be rearranged. However, it is somewhat embarrassing to have to return to the listing office to move the First Appointment if your own client cannot make the date.

3.04 Although under the Pilot Scheme District Judges have been fairly sympathetic to releasing parties from attendance at the First Appointment, this may well change if there is a trend, as expected, to a increased use of those appointments as FDRs.

3.05 Similarly, if you file a number of Forms A at the same time, you will find that you have a closely bunched group of First Appointments. It is not impossible, particularly in the larger courts, to have two First Appointments not only on the same day, but also at the same time! This provides an obvious logistical difficulty, but there are potential problems even if the appointments are not on the same day. Three or four first Appointments within two or three days of each other mean that all the deadlines for the exchange of Forms E and filing of Questionnaires and requests for documents, chronologies and Statements of Issues will also occur at around the same time. As there is inevitably a scramble to finalise these documents (and do not deceive yourself that life in this respect will be any different under the Amended Rules), you will find yourself with major headaches if you fail to stagger the filing of Forms A. And do not forget that practitioners on the other side may be about to file on behalf of their clients. With a little bad luck, and some careless filing on your own part, you could easily end up with seven or eight First Appointments in the space of a few days, which is not to be recommended.

3.06 One tip if you find yourself in two consecutive First Appointments before different judges in the same court. Ask the listing department to re-list them consecutively in front of the same judge. This eliminates a hasty scramble between courtrooms, and ensures that you will not be late for the second hearing if the first overruns.

3.07 This leads to the question of who should file their application first. Now that the court controls the timetable of the application from beginning to end, the decision is often less important than it was under the old system. However, if you think that there is a chance of the case fighting, do you want to have the opening submission or not at the final hearing? If so, file first. You may also find it a useful tool when conducting voluntary negotiations. A timely application, giving you a backstop date if negotiations flounder, can be very useful for concentrating everyone's minds.

A note about Form B

3.08 An application for ancillary relief may also be started by the issue of Form B, which replaces the old Form M12[1]. In Rule 2.45(5), the reference to Rules 2.62(3) to (7) should be replaced by the new Rules 2.51B to 2.70. Thereafter, within the new rules, all references to Form A should be taken as if they were references to Form B.

1 Rule 5(1).

The Procedure following the filing of Form A

3.09 Under the Pilot Scheme, the court provided the applicant with the Notice of First Appointment, and the applicant had then to serve the respondent with a copy, together with a copy of Form A. The Amended Rules provide that the court must now serve the Notice (the new Form C), and the copy Form A *within four days of the filing of the notice*[1]. What happens, though, to the application if the court fails to meet this time limit? If courts are inefficient, and Form C is served out of time, what will be the result? Are the proceedings invalid because the procedure has not been complied with? If Form C is served late, the applicant's solicitors should try the following steps:

1   try writing to the other party's solicitors. Ask them to confirm that they will treat the First Appointment as effective in any event. (The other side may not play ball: after all, *should* a solicitor bind his client to accept a shorter than prescribed time for completion of his Form E? If the Form cannot then be completed in time, and the court imposes a cost penalty, has the solicitor been negligent?) To avoid negligence, it appears that in reply to an invitation to treat the First Appointment as effective, the client's position should be reserved.

2   if on the receiving end of such a reservation, an alternative solution might be to apply to a judge to re-list the First Appointment to give the full time for the preparation of Form E. Presumably it would be difficult for the Respondent's solicitors to resist such an application if they are not prepared to confirm that the First Appointment will be effective.

3   Don't simply ignore the problem. If the First Appointment is ineffective, the Applicant's solicitors could be negligent if they have not spotted, and made appropriate representations about, the procedural irregularity.

1   Rule 2.61A(4)(a), (b).

3.10   Practitioners used to the Pilot Scheme's Notice of First Appointment will be pleased to see that the amended notice in Form C states the 'no later than' dates on its face. Under the Pilot Scheme, the calculation of those dates was made by the applicant and then confirmed in correspondence. There was debate within ARAG about whether Disclosure should be given earlier than before, to allow more time for negotiation before the First Appointment. This seemed especially a possibility as the amended Rules were to provide for a longer run up to the First Appointment (12 to 14 weeks) from the filing of Form A than under the Pilot Scheme (10 to 12 weeks). In the event, this change did not take place: perhaps it was decided that the additional time would be needed to complete the additional discovery which will have to be made under the Amended Rules before the First Appointment.

3.11   Once the date of a First, or any subsequent, Appointment has been fixed, it can only be cancelled with leave of the court. If leave is given, the court must immediately re-fix the appointment for a new date[1]. This appears to be part of the Lord Chancellor's Department's determination that cases proceed expeditiously, quickly and efficiently. Practitioners should make it clear to their clients that, one an application has been commenced, barring quite exceptional circumstances, it will move inexorably forward to a final resolution in court.

1   Rule 2.61A(5).

CHAPTER 4 – PREPARATION FOR THE FIRST APPOINTMENT

What must be done?

4.01   There are five steps which must be completed before the First Appointment:

1   No later than 35 days before the First Appointment, a pro forma financial statement must be completed by each party in Form E, and must be sworn to be

true. Prescribed documents must be annexed to the Form E and it must be filed and exchanged with the other party.

2   No later than 14 days before the First Appointment, each party must file and serve a concise statement of the issues in the case, a chronology and either a Questionnaire referring to the concise statement of issues, together with a schedule of required documents, or a statement that further information is not required.

3   No later than 14 days before the First Appointment, each party must file and serve a notice in Form G stating whether the party will be in a position to use all or part of the First Appointment as an FDR.

4   No later than 14 days before the First Appointment, the applicant must file and serve on the respondent confirmation that Rule 2.70(4) has been complied with (if appropriate) and confirmation that every person who should be served with notice of the application under Rule 2.59(3) and (4) has been served.

5   At the First Appointment, each party must produce to the court in Form H an estimate of the costs incurred up to the date of the First Appointment.

Preparing Form E

4.02   The narrative affidavit is dead. Long live Form E. The demise of the narrative affidavit has disappointed many practitioners, who consider that they are being robbed of the opportunity to vent fully their clients' cases. However, given the demise of 'conduct' in all but exceptional cases, and as Form E enables each party to comment on conduct and lifestyle issues, it is arguable that nothing significant is lost. The fact that Form E ensures that all information is provided in the same format by all parties makes it much easier for judges and practitioners alike to find specific financial details in any case. It also ensures that, so far as possible, no relevant information is inadvertently omitted.

4.03   The template Form E which is appended to the Amended Rules is a considerable improvement on the original, which formed part of the Pilot Scheme. It is, as yet, unclear which software companies will dominate the market with a 'Form E package'. Programmers were, understandably, unwilling to devote significant resources to create a perfect package for the Pilot Scheme when: (*a*) the scheme might never be rolled out; and (*b*), even if it was introduced nationally, there might be such significant changes as to render a program unadaptable.

Which Form E?

4.04   The majority of practitioners working with the Pilot Scheme have found, as far as we can tell, that a Form E which adds in additional pages of information with a page number suffix (eg 'page 8(a)'), is preferred by judges to those which simply expand the form by continuing the page numbering. Put shortly, judges appear to be happier knowing that, for example, page 10 will always be 'pension', and page 15 'income needs', however many pages (a) and (b) have been added in, than to find pensions eventually on page 18, because an additional eight pages have been inserted before them. An alternative to these methods would be to make any continuations on appendix sheets at the end of the Form. These, though, would form part of the sworn statement, and should therefore be attached before the jurat on page 20, rather than simply 'attached to it' as the prescribed documents should be.

Filling in Form E

Part 1 General Information

4.05   Questions 1.1 to 1.6 are unexceptional, but question 1.7 could cause confusion if the client has become engaged, but has not yet set a date for re-marriage. The Form does not, we submit, put such a client under an obligation to make immediate marriage plans, so mark the box 'not yet set', and tick the appropriate responses at question 1.8 and 1.9

4.06   'Children of the family' at 1.10 should include just children who are children of the marriage or have been treated as children of the family. Presumably the 'children' referred to at 1.11 are similarly 'children of the family'. If, therefore, a party finds him or herself looking after a sick child (perhaps from a former relationship) who is not a child of the family, then that child should not be included here. If relevant, and it may be, this situation should be recorded as one of 'any other circumstances which…could affect the extent of the financial provision to be made…' at question 4.5 on page 18 of the Form. When completing the answer to question 1.11, it would be helpful to add the words 'but see also the reply to 4.5 at page 18' at the foot of the box.

The most common difficulties which arise with question 1.12, the present and future arrangements for the education of the children, are either the possibility that the children may have to move schools because of a geographical move by the parent with care following a financial settlement, or the removal of children from the private sector as a result of the separation of finances after divorce. If either of these are the case, simply explain the potential difficulties to the court, continuing (we suggest) onto 'page 3(a)' if necessary. For example:

Present arrangements	Future arrangements
Jack is currently at Blackdown Preparatory School, Shropshire; Jill is at Homewood Abbey School Gloucestershire.	*The petitioner hopes that Jack will stay at Blackdown until he is 13, and then move to Stowe, and that Jill will continue at Homewood Abbey. If this cannot be afforded, the children may have to be removed from the private sector and go to Oswestry Comprehensive.*

Or:

Present arrangements	Future arrangements
Jack is currently at Blackdown Preparatory School, Shropshire; Jill is at Homewood Abbey School, Gloucestershire.	*The petitioner hopes that these arrangements will continue. If however, she cannot afford to stay in the vicinity of the Former Matrimonial Home, she intends to move to Lancashire, and will look for appropriate schools for Jack and Jill at that time.*

4.07   It may, of course, be tactically better to make no admission that there is any question that the children may be changing schools. This will depend on how the case is being conducted.

4.08   Question 1.13, which asks for details of maintenance agreements or orders for children, or an estimate of the liability of a non-resident parent under the Child Support Act, is new since the Pilot Scheme was introduced. We anticipate that, at least unless and until the changes to the Child Support Act envisaged by the current White Paper come into force, many practitioners will make any calculations of child support using a proprietary computer program. If so, although the calculations need not accompany Form E, it may be as well to include them, as the Rules permit 'to explain or clarify...the information'[1]. The Rules are silent about how an applicant mother with care is expected to provide such an estimate before she has sight of the absent father's financial disclosure, in cases where she has no idea of his financial circumstances, but then 'estimate' is a helpfully elastic word.

1   Rule 2.61(B)(3)(b).

4.09   Questions 1.14, 1.15 and 1.16 are, similarly, all additions since the Pilot Scheme and are self-explanatory. Question 1.14 requires narrative, and may require an additional page or pages. However, given the spirit of the scheme, try to avoid producing the equivalent of an old style affidavit. Confine the client to the actual changes which have taken place since the order was made. Identify those changes with clear references to the appropriate passages or sections of the parties' affidavits of means or Forms E as the case may be, as these will still be on the court file.

Question 1.16 is presumably designed to avoid the confusion which could arise when completing the original Form E if the parties owned property, but rented the Matrimonial Home, or occupied it under some other arrangement.

Part 2 Financial Details

Property interests

4.10   Questions 2.1 and 2.2 deal with property interests. The note at the top of page 4 requires a copy of a valuation to be attached, if one has been obtained in the last six months, together with a copy of the most recent mortgage statement. Confusingly, the asterisk which alerts the reader to this note relates only to the column marked 'property value' at question 2.1, and not to the same column in question 2.2. However, on the front of Form E, there is clear instruction that the *'Essential documents'* which *'must'* accompany [the] Statement, are detailed at questions 2.1, *2.2*, 2.3...' [our italics]. Clearly it is intended that recent valuations of <u>all</u> property in the case should be produced. We also consider that, as the Form envisages the possibility of multiple mortgages, presumably the italicised instruction should read 'a copy of your most recent mortgage statement (or statements) is/are also required'. We strongly recommend that you provide all these documents. In the highly unlikely event that a judge should criticise you for not sticking to the letter of the request in the Form, you may point, with justification, to Rule 2.61B(3)(b), and argue that the additional documents are 'necessary to explain or clarify' the information given in response to question 2.2, and therefore 'must' be attached. Curiously, Form E itself on page one only states that such clarifying information 'may' be attached.

4.11   A word about valuations. The purpose of requiring the prescribed documents to accompany Form E is to attempt to cover the standard reasonable and appropriate requests for disclosure which would be included in the average request for documents accompanying a questionnaire at a First Appointment. ARAG realised that, if sufficient discovery could be provided before the First Appointment, then in a reasonably straightforward case it might well be possible to conduct serious negotiations shortly after the exchange of Forms E and use the First Appointment as an FDR. Valuations of property will, in most cases, be fundamental to the negotiations. You may well not need a full, formal valuation. In many cities and towns where there is a fast turnover of properties of a similar type, an Estate Agent's 'asking price' valuation from each side may well enable the question of valuation to be agreed. The Rules are quite clear. If you do not already have a valuation less than six months old, you do not have to obtain one, and your client may instead give their own estimate. However, unless you have a good tactical reason for slowing negotiations down, why not advise your client to obtain such a valuation in any event? The valuation should be an informal one and in order to avoid the costs of duplication and difficulties when a formal valuation may be required, an attempt should be made to agree the identity of the valuer jointly and to instruct them with the co-operation of the other spouse's solicitors.

4.12   One question which arises occasionally is whether 'timeshares' constitute property, and should therefore be included in the reply to question 2.2, or are construed as an 'other realisable asset' more appropriately listed at 2.11. This may be a matter of personal preference. Ours is for an inclusion as property in 2.2, but we consider that practitioners are unlikely to be criticised for taking the alternative view. There are clients whose experience of these schemes suggests to them that section 2.12 'liabilities' would be a more appropriate listing for timeshares. Certainly there may be a point to remember here when considering capital gains and losses for the reply to question 2.13.

Bank accounts

4.13   Question 2.3 asks for details of all bank, building society and National Savings accounts, together with PEPs, TESSAs and ISAs. For those who find it convenient to list all bank accounts together, regardless of whether they are in credit or overdrawn, the requirement to list overdrawn accounts in the 'liabilities' section at 2.12 is irksome. There seems to be no reason why all the accounts should not be *listed* at any rate at section 2.3, with the total left blank for those accounts which are in overdraft, and a note referring the reader to section 2.12, where those accounts can be listed again. Given the amount of information required in box 2.3, the space available is very limited. You may be able to squeeze it in by reducing the font size; otherwise run onto two or three lines per account, and use an additional page if necessary.

4.14   *Note the requirement for bank statements for each account for the last twelve months*. Fortunately, duplicate bank statements are now reasonably cheap to obtain but, added to the other prescribed documents, they can mean a lot of paper. There is also a degree of absurdity in requiring both parties to produce a year's worth of statements on a number of joint bank accounts, which is what the rules actually require. Only time and experience will show whether judges are happy to accept the provision of such statements by just one party, if this is agreed by the other.

Securities

4.15   Question 2.4 deals with stocks and shares, and *share based* PEPs and ISAs. Beware of using portfolio valuations which were prepared by brokers some months ago, particularly if the portfolio is diversified. As the 'dotcom' feeding frenzy of recent months has proved, niche market shares can move up and down very rapidly. Try to value portfolios as near to the swear date of Form E as possible, and add a note to box 2.4 with the valuation date. Changing *any* value at the last minute if you are producing Form E in a standard word processing package is irritating and time-consuming. Not only must you correct the total in the relevant box, but you then have to move that calculation forward as part of at least two other calculations, leaving plenty of scope for arithmetical errors. The new generation of self-calculating forms should resolve that particular problem, but if you are doing the job manually, make sure you leave plenty of time to check and re-check the calculations.

Insurance policies

4.16   The gloss to question 2.5 is a helpful addition to the Pilot Scheme Form E. The original Form did not make it clear that policies with no surrender value – principally 'whole life' policies – should be included. As a result, given the box marked 'surrender value' within the table, many practitioners assumed that, as life policies had no true value, they should be omitted. However, given that security for maintenance is frequently a significant stumbling block, life policies can be a vital part of negotiations. Full details about them might mean the difference between concluding a deal at a First Appointment (because it can be treated as an FDR) and not. *Note the requirement to attach any surrender value quotations to the Form.*

National Savings and debtors

4.17   Questions 2.6 and 2.7 deal with the various forms of National Savings, and are self-explanatory. The difference between 'current value' and 'total current value of your interest' arises, as elsewhere in the Form, where the holdings are in joint names. Question 2.8 asks for your debtors, and the level of those debts. Although these are assets, and there is therefore a requirement to disclose them, they can be somewhat misleading. Directors' accounts may or may not be liquid, either in part or in full. Partners' loan accounts, for example, within firms of solicitors, rarely are. Debts owed by private individuals may or may not be worth the paper they are written on. And remember, gambling debts are not enforceable. Do not shrink from adding glosses to the figures, both in this box and at the end of the form. The total in each box will form part of the final total, and you must be mindful of using the final 'net asset' figure if along the way there have been sub-totals which call for more thoughtful interpretation.

Cash and chattels

4.18   Question 2.9 in its original form in the Pilot Scheme's Form E had no limit. This led to parties either estimating the amount of the cash float which they usually carried around in their pockets or purses, or emptying out their loose change on their solicitor's desk when they came to swear the Form. Significant cash holdings are comparatively rare, but they can occur, for example, with self employed car dealers or antique dealers, and even with professional gamblers.

4.19 Chattels, at question 2.10 cause numerous problems. There are parties who have not been inside the former matrimonial home for so long that they cannot remember precisely what is there. Others will either wildly over- or under-value furniture and paintings, especially if they think that the other is likely to retain them. It is usually the case that most 'new' furniture is worth but a fraction of what was paid for it. Antiques only reach their purchase price after a number of years, and jewellery can usually comfortably be written down at about a third of the insurance replacement value. Motor cars, too, have suffered recently as a result of the continuing drive by manufacturers to ensure lower and lower forecourt prices for new machines. An up-to-date used car price guide is therefore a worthwhile addition to the practitioner's bookshelf: as with most chattels, the car owner's estimate of its value can be woefully wide of the mark.

4.20 Cars, the Form states, shall be included at section 2.10 at 'gross value'. If there is any car specific HP, or similar financing arrangement, then include the outstanding debt in the 'liabilities' section at 2.12. Do remember that there are currently a number of financing schemes available which operate on a semi-lease basis. Ordinarily, these schemes demand a deposit, followed by a series of deceptively low monthly payments, and then a large final payment at the end of the contract (typically two or three years). Midway through the term, particularly with less popular models, many clients may actually have 'negative equity' in their cars as a result of these schemes.

Other realisable assets

4.21 Question 2.12 deals with as yet unlisted *realisable* assets, rather than illiquid assets, like share options, business assets and pensions, which are dealt with later. The inclusion of business expansion schemes therefore seems curious. These schemes typically are not immediately realisable, and so may be more appropriately listed at section 2.17. It is important to separate out liquid and illiquid assets, if only to give a judge a clear indication of what may practically be divided. However, although the total boxes at page 14 provide totals with and without pensions, they do not at any point exclude other illiquid assets, an important point to bear in mind if the other party starts talking about percentages of assets.

If you are completing the Form manually, take care with the following calculation not to add in the value of the former matrimonial home, if it has one. This is section (A), and is counted separately.

Liabilities

4.22 Questions 2.12 and 2.13 deal with liabilities and potential Capital Gains Tax respectively. Both are straightforward to complete, although with clients whose financial affairs are complicated, the calculation of any potential CGT liability may require the assistance of an accountant to calculate it. If this is the case, it would be sensible to include the calculation of that liability as an additional document, as the Rules permit, to explain and clarify the figure.

Loans from parents, family and friends may be included at section 2.12, but bear in mind that without documentation to the contrary, they are likely to be treated by the court as 'soft' loans, the repayment of which is not pressing. The exception to this rule of thumb will be where some unforeseen event has made the repayment pressing (for example the illness of the lender). If this is the case, footnote the fact.

When changing any figures as a result of further information from your client while in the process of completing the Form, remember to keep updating totals (C) and (D) on page 8, if you are completing the Form manually.

Business assets

4.23   These are only of interest where there is a private company, a partnership or a sole trader in the case. Directors of publicly quoted companies who have an interest will disclose their shareholdings in section 2.4. Note that no formal valuation is required at this stage. Remember that in many cases, the value of a business which is the principal income producing asset in the case has a largely academic interest unless there is a serious chance of it being sold or floated. Remember the dictum of Booth J in *Evans* v *Evans*[1]:

> 'While it may be necessary to obtain a broad assessment of the value of a shareholding in a private company, it is inappropriate to undertake an expensive and meaningless exercise to achieve a precise valuation of a private company which will not be sold'

1   [1990] 1 FLR 319.

4.24   There are three principal competing methods for a 'rule of thumb' valuation of a party's interest in a private company. The first two, the so called 'asset value' and the 'dividend yield value' are of less value to a family lawyer than the third, the 'earnings basis valuation'. For the roughest of calculations, do the following exercise (which derives from At A Glance):

1   Take the last three years' gross profits. Adjust them by adding back inappropriate payments (like very large pension contributions) or by deducting exceptional 'one off' income. Multiply the most recent year's profits by three, the next most recent by two and the final year by one. Add the totals of these calculations together and divide the resulting sum by six. This gives an average of profits weighted to the company's most recent performance, and is described at the 'maintainable earnings' of the business.

2   Multiply the maintainable earnings figure by the Profits:Earnings ratio (rounded down to the nearest whole number) for the type of business which is being valued. This may be found in the daily Financial Times Actuaries Share Index.

3   Discount for the size of the business. Again, this is designed only as a rough rule of thumb. Take the earnings of the business and multiply by the relevant percentage:

Profit in £s	*Percentage multiplier*
More than 1,000,000	100%
500,000 – 1,000,000	90%
250,000 – 500,00	80%
100,000 – 250,000	66%
less than 100,000	50%

4   Now discount for the control of the shareholder:

Percentage of voting shares	*Percentage multiplier*
More than 75%	100%
51% - 75%	85%

50%	75%
25% - 49%	65%
10% - 25%	55%
less than 10%	45%

4.25 Remember that result achieved by this calculation is illusory, in the sense that shares in private businesses cannot be traded like houses or motor cars. However, it provides a reasonable estimate of value for the purposes of Form E.

As with CGT calculations, it is probably worth including the workings of your calculations when you file and serve Form E. Indeed, if those workings can be described as a 'document', then they *must* be included. Such a calculations are only really of value if the business to which they relate is unlikely to be sold. Otherwise professional valuations are likely to be sought, and directions to this effect will be given at the First Appointment. Of course, if a party has a valuation which he or she has recently had prepared (perhaps for the benefit of bankers) it should be attached, and there is nothing to prevent a party from commissioning one for the purpose of proceedings before being ordered to do so. This may be a question of tactics. It may be something that the party who is not involved in the business will decide to do upon receipt of two years accounts. *Note the requirement to attach the last two years' accounts to the Form.*

4.26 Question 2.15 requires a list of directorships for the last twelve months. For parties with a large number of directorships, the swiftest and most economical response will probably be to append to the Form the standard list produced by Companies House which is available over the internet for a modest fee.

Pensions

4.27 Few pages of Form E strike terror into client and practitioner alike as efficiently as page 10, containing question 2.16 about pension details. Who among us who have practised the Pilot Scheme have not wrestled with countless pages of material from a client's pension provider, trying to reduce it all to the elegant form required by page 10? Here's a tip. In the first instance, don't try. Simply send off to each pension provider, including those dealing with AVCs and FURBs, as early as possible the following:
(i)   a signed letter of authorisation from your client to provide you with any information you may require;
(ii)   a blank copy of page 10 of Form E for every pension with that provider; and
(iii)   a letter from you to the pension provider asking them to complete the Form and stressing the urgency with which the information is required.

4.28 It usually works. There are some less helpful providers who simply send you back their standard pack of information, but this usually has sufficient information concealed within to enable you to complete the page. The important thing is to start the process off early as early as possible. Pension companies are not, in our experience, particularly swift in providing this information. Make the initial request a couple of weeks before issuing Form A. Once you have a date for the First Appointment, write to them again explaining that the question is now urgent, as you have an imminent court appointment, for which your mutual client is required to provide the information. If after another couple of weeks has passed you have still heard nothing, a very charming but slightly desperate telephone call usually does the trick.

4.29   We hasten to point out that this is not simply the lazy practitioner's approach. It is far cheaper for the client to ask the pension providers to do the work, rather than for you to sift through the enormous quantities of chaff supplied for the wheat that you need. Furthermore, if there is anything which is unclear when the completed page returns to you, there is usually a contact name with it, and anyone regularly dealing with large organisations knows that this is manna. *Remember that you will need the pension valuation document from the pension provider in any event, as this must accompany Form E.*

4.30   In the majority of cases, the most important questions about pensions are the size of the CETV and the potential widow's benefit that will be lost on divorce. Earmarking cases remain comparatively uncommon, and only when pension splitting becomes a live issue is this position likely to change.

Other assets

4.31   Include in section 2.17 any asset which does not seem to fit into any of the other categories. The Form mentions unrealisable assets, share option schemes and trust interests. What exactly *are* unrealisable assets? Woe betide anyone, we presume, who lists 'good looks and charm'. Examples could include a share in a house subject to the life interest of, perhaps, a parent or other family member, or a share in a something unusual, like a racing car, which it may be virtually impossible to sell outside the group of co-owners concerned. Share options always present a difficulty. Section 2.17 tells you to state 'the estimated net sale proceeds if the options were capable of exercise now', but share options are not 'exercisable now': that's their point. There are two problems here. First, it is impossible to say with certainty how the strike price will compare with the option price in, say, three years' time. Secondly, even if it were, should there not be some discount for the fact that the funds will not, in any event, be available for three years? Presumably the best approach is to complete section 2.17 exactly as the Form requires, but to add a clear note to the effect that the total figure is potentially misleading. This could be re-enforced in section 4.5 (which does specifically mention contingent liabilities) if you think that there is any danger of the judge missing the point.

4.32   As far as trust interests are concerned, in all but the simplest trusts, take advantage of the opportunity afforded by the Amended Rules to attach '… other documents necessary to explain or clarify the information contained…'. Do, though, add some narrative at section 2.17. The other party's solicitors will wish to trawl through the minutiae of the trust provisions. The judge at the First Appointment or the FDR will not.

Income

4.33   The questions at 2.18 relating to earned income are usually comparatively straightforward to answer. The requirement by the Rules to provide the last three payslips and P60 prompt the client to provide them in a more timely fashion than is sometimes the case when a financial affidavit is being drafted. Bear in mind that the Amended Rules will not change the following fact. However stable and successful a party's employment, he or she will almost certainly work on the basis that they will receive no pay rise and no bonus for the coming year, no matter what the historical position shows. If this really does appear to be the case, then it will need to be explained at least in a footnote. It would also be appropriate to include a letter or memorandum from an employer explaining the current position. This is also true in the case of management buyouts, imminent take-overs and major company re-structuring.

4.34 The greatest problem with earned income usually arises where the client is working abroad. They may be paid in sterling into a UK account, or locally, or to some tax haven, either in whole or in part. There may be allowances paid at different rates of exchange for different purposes. For example, certain EU employees are permitted to remit a proportion of their salaries (which are paid in Euros) to their home nations at a highly favourable rate of exchange, provided that they have a good reason for so doing. The maintenance of a home, maintenance to a child at university, school fees and spousal maintenance would all fall within this category. In our experience, expatriate workers are not always completely clear themselves about how their remuneration package works. If there is any doubt, arm yourself with your client's authority and speak direct to the employer. Get confirmation of everything in writing, and attach this memorandum or letter to Form E.

4.35 Some clients' income comes from multiple sources. For example he may be a director of two or three companies, have a flourishing self-employed career as a journalist, and also have some royalty income from a couple of novels. Remember to separate the income out into the relevant sections (in the above case, sections 2.18, 2.20 and 2.23, respectively). In a very complex case, it will probably be helpful to present a summary of the income on one sheet of A4 paper, and attach it to the Form by way of clarification.

4.36 For earned income, the financial year is the tax year, ie the year to 5 April. Practitioners who have worked with the Pilot Scheme will notice the clarification of the requirement for the current year's income. The original Form E did not specify that income for the current year should be extrapolated to cover the whole of that year, and many people considered, not unreasonably, that the question meant 'year to date'. The figures were fairly obvious if they were entered just a few months into the new financial year. However, a Form E completed in the early months of a calendar year, following a significant pay rise could cause considerable confusion. *Note the requirement to attach the last three payslips and the P60 for the most recently completed financial year to the Form.*

Additional income: benefits, etc

4.37 Given the requirement for payslips and P60, it is surprising that the Rules do not require a copy P11D. It is helpful to ask the client to provide one or two of these, and there seems to us to be no reason why one should not be provided with Form E alongside the P60, particularly if there are significant benefits. The most usual benefits and perks include private health cover, pension contributions and the company car. There may also be allowances for mobile telephones, subsistence allowances and expense accounts, the latter especially for those who are seconded abroad, or who travel extensively. There is a significant difference between subsistence allowances, which are paid in any event, and the reclaiming of expenses once they have been paid. Reimbursement of expenses should be looked at carefully as the 'expense account effect' may reduce the party's reasonable needs.

Self-employed or partnership income

4.38   Like much of Form E, the new section 2.20, relating to self-employed or partnership income is greatly improved from the earlier incarnation. The period for annual profit and loss is specified, as is what the expressions 'year 1' and 'year 2' relate to. Provided you have two years' accounts from your client, completing this section should be plain sailing. There, of course, is the rub. Sadly there are many occasions when self-employed clients decline to waste good money on accountants. Take the case of the used car dealer of foreign origin. He travelled every six weeks or so, first to the north of continental Europe, where he purchased his stock. Then, having shipped it south to his native continent, he set about selling it. He kept no accounts, nor indeed did he have a bank account for trading. All transactions, he said, were in cash. He was unclear how much he earned from his endeavours. His first guess at a net income proved to be less than he was paying in interim maintenance and school fees, and so was less than helpful. In the end, his long suffering solicitor tried to extrapolate an annual income from a typical buying and selling trip, and cross reference this to the client's expenditure, taking into account the handmade suits and the new and very expensive German car parked outside the office. No judge is likely to be impressed, but there is little more you can do in circumstances like these.

4.39   Another difficulty arises when dealing with clients who are partners in firms of solicitors. Here it is easy to confirm the previous years' drawings, and to make a reasonably accurate estimate of the drawings for the current year. But what about distribution of undrawn profits? Frequently there will be elements of undrawn profits from a number of previous years. Firms' drawings policies in relation to undrawn profits can vary widely from year to year, depending on cashflow, expansion plans and just plain poor performance. The best approach is to complete section 2.20 including undrawn profit simply as part of the client's 'share of profit/loss', and then write a careful additional note. This note should also be related to box 2.24 – the estimate of the current year's net income, more about which see below. ***Note the requirement to attach accounts for the last two accounting years***.

Investment income

4.40   Question 2.21 requires a schedule of investment income, stating whether it is paid gross or net, but *not* requiring the client to calculate any tax payable that may arise. Why not? This seems a curious exception, given the lengths to which parties are expected to go to calculate other relevant deductions, like potential CGT. Besides, how can a client make an 'estimate of [his] current annual net income from all sources', for section 2.24 without such an estimate? The obvious solution is simply to calculate the tax. The Form says 'you are not required to…', not 'you are required not to…'. Otherwise the procedure would be to enter the figure as requested in box 2.21, and then calculate the tax for any investment income and deduct this from total income before putting that figure in section 2.24, adding a footnote to explain what has been done. Then, if you have a computer program which automatically totals boxes 2.18 to 2.23, amend it manually if need be, and remember that you have done so if you subsequently amend any of the individual income totals.

Any other income

4.41   Similarly, question 2.23, which requires details of any other income, for example royalties and trust income, does not state whether the figure is to be given gross or net. Bearing in mind the above, why not give the net figure?

Summary of your income

4.42   The left-hand box is simply the total of boxes 2.18 to 2.23, with the caveats above. The right-hand box, though, requires some crystal ball gazing. Try to steer the client away from the wilder shores of excess when bemoaning his or her prospects. Remember that any reduction in income between the current year and the next requires explanation. This may be done appropriately at section 4.5, but a one-line footnote would do no harm here. Bear in mind that while you may well be able to include a note in the left-hand box, the right-hand one may be part of your program's self-calculating mechanism, and resist the inclusion of text. If so, many programs permit notes on a following page, or even directly under the box itself. Thus the final response to section 2.24 might appear as follows:

2.24   Summary of your income

Your estimate of your current annual net from all sources (2.18 – 2.23)	Your estimate of your net income from all income sources for the next 52 weeks*
£ 40,300 *This total includes a deduction of £ 400 from the total in box 2.21 for the additional incidence of income tax at 15% over the tax deducted at basic rate.*	**£38,300** **(J)**

*The Respondent anticipates a net salary increase of £4,000 for next year, but that his royalty income will fall by £6,000 net for the same period.

Summary of financial information

4.43   Those practitioners who have struggled through the Pilot Scheme with inadequate word processing-based Forms E will welcome the new generation of self-calculating Forms which are finding their way onto the market. Remember how frequently last-minute amendments are made to affidavits. Form E is no different. It is remarkably easy to engross and corner a Form E ready for swearing, having just updated a list of share prices, and then realise that although the totals at (B3) on page 5, and **B** on page 14 have been amended, **(B)** on page 7 has been overlooked and is now wrong.

Part 3 Requirements

Income needs

4.44   Increasingly, practitioners have a pro-forma schedule for income requirements, which they hand to clients at an early stage in proceedings and ask them to complete in draft. There has been a vogue among many Pilot Scheme practitioners to attach a final version of such a schedule to the Form E, simply putting the relevant totals on the form itself. Whether this practice continues may depend on the quality of the Form E programs which come onto the market. It may, for example, prove possible to customise page 15 and some addendum pages as a 'stand alone' document like the kind of schedules which are currently used, and which can simply be incorporated back into the Form once they have been finalised. The advantage of this method would be the immediate incorporation of any last minute amendments. If the new programs prove less flexible, however, the earlier method may continue. We have not heard it criticised by any judges during the currency of the Pilot Scheme.

4.45   There is a practice among some practitioners, when working on 'high income' cases, to omit the income requirements of the paying party (most frequently the husband). The omission is made ostensibly on the ground that it is not necessary to give the information because the payer will be able to provide any amount of maintenance which the court could reasonably order. This practice is questionable: the real motive behind it appears to be to avoid the necessity of the payer demonstrating his own spending patterns, and a comparison with those claimed by the payee as reasonable. How could a husband rail against his wife's proposed expenditure of £10,000 a year for holidays, when he spends £40,000? Experience has shown that judges, at least for the most part, have turned a blind eye to this practice. Whether all courts will do so is a matter for conjecture. One danger of following this practice is that it becomes tempting to continue it further down the financial ladder. It may be arguable that if a man has an income of £1m a year, his income requirements are irrelevant. To argue the same when his income is £100,000 a year (as we have seen done) is dangerous and could, we consider, lead to a penalty in costs at a First Appointment if the judge considers that failure to complete this section has hampered negotiations.

4.46   Although the Form states that figures may be expressed weekly, monthly or annually, provided that the period used is consistent, experience suggests that judges are most used to thinking in terms of an annual income, and it is therefore probably best to stick to annual figures on the Form. However, clients are frequently more at home working in shorter periods for certain expenditure: most people seem to think in terms of weekly figures for food and petrol, monthly for loan repayments and annually for clothes and holidays. Let them jumble everything together if they wish. There is probably less room for error if everything is standardised at the time it is finalised and incorporated into the Form.

4.47   Don't forget that what the Form asks for is an estimate of 'the reasonable *future* income needs…'. If the client is going to move to a smaller property, remember to scale down running costs from their current levels.

4.48   The Pilot Scheme's Form E allowed only for the income needs of children 'living with you'. The new Form includes the wording '…or provided for by you…' What this term is intended to encompass is not entirely clear. Is it the money which an absent parent wishes to spend on his children when he has contact with them, or which he spends on children from another relationship for whom he is already paying maintenance? Equally, is it expenditure on the needs of other children for whom voluntary provision is made – perhaps the provision of a godchild's school fees? The answer seems to be 'if in doubt, put it in'. All these points would need to be made somewhere, and hitherto the only place on the Form was 'Other Information'. It seems sensible to gather everything about children together in one section.

Capital needs

4.49   In probably the majority of cases, this centres on the provision of a new home or the wished-for retention by the parent with care of the children of the former matrimonial home. Again, take advantage of the provision enabling the inclusion of '… other documents necessary to explain or clarify the information contained…', to exhibit appropriate property particulars. Don't forget to include the cost of moving, and any decorating, re-carpeting and re-equipping which may be required. There may be enough furniture in the former matrimonial home to furnish two smaller properties. If the wife intends to stay put, though, the husband may need to start largely from scratch.

4.50 If the wife *is* to stay put, her other capital needs may be higher than they would be if she were to move. Frequently where a relationship is breaking down maintenance of the home and updating of its contents becomes neglected. Judges may be unimpressed by claims for *Besterman* cushions, but they may be moved by the urgent need for a new washing machine and a new boiler. And why not include with Form E a brief report from the man who services these appliances? It may not provide compelling evidence of a need, but it is better than nothing.

4.51 Don't forget to look at the state of the party's car. A replacement may represent capital expenditure, unless it is fairly new, in which case it is likely to be covered within the figure which has been given in the 'Income needs' section, which should include depreciation. Essentially, any particularly aged equipment should be looked at as potential capital expenditure when completing Form E. From a 'client care', the 'wish list' created in the requirements section of Form E is often more obvious than it is in a narrative affidavit. Be careful to warn the client about the practicalities, especially as you may have only the sketchiest idea of the other party's financial position.

4.52 Children's capital needs are frequently covered within those of the parent with care. However, increasingly the need for computer equipment is recognised, and in wealthier families there may be other 'necessities', like ponies, mopeds, mobile telephones and even motor cars. The needs of children with disabilities should not be overlooked.

Part 4 Other Information

Significant changes in net assets

4.53 Question 4.1, which asks for details of any significant change in net assets during the last twelve months, is an addition to the original Form, but its purpose seems confused. It gives as an example the closure of any bank or building society accounts, an example which seems unhelpful. If the Form is trying to find out whether there has been dissipation, it should ask the question more directly. Information about the movement of funds from, or closure of, accounts in the preceding twelve months will be available from the statements, which must be attached. What would be more helpful is a summary of changes to such accounts, cross-referenced to the statements. What the question actually seems to be asking for is, for example, a very significant rise in the value of properties owned, or stocks held. This may have a relevance to 'contribution' when looking at the 'section 25 factors', but it is difficult to see that it will take negotiations much further in any other way.

Standard of living

4.54 It should be clear from the size of the box at question 4.2, which deals with standard of living during the marriage, that practitioners are not being invited to slip in a narrative affidavit. Keep it short, concentrating on the practical financial aspects: the type of houses the parties lived in, and the progression from house to house. If appropriate, the length, frequency and financial level of holidays, the type, cost and frequency with which they ate out or entertained. Look at cars, clothes and hobbies. An example for an applicant wife might read as follows:

4.2 Give brief details of the standard of living enjoyed by you and your spouse during the marriage

We have lived comfortably throughout our marriage, and our standard of living has been particularly high in the last eight years since the Respondent became managing director of Tubthumpers Limited. When we were first married we lived in a four-bedroom house in Esher; but we moved five years ago to our current home in Weybridge, which has six bedroom suites and an acre of gardens, with a swimming pool. We have always taken two foreign holidays as a family each year and for the last six years have flown club class, and stayed at five star 'resort' hotels. The Respondent and I have spent four or five weekends a year in Country House hotels for the last five or six years, and we eat out once or twice a week at the best restaurants in Weybridge, frequently entertaining friends at those restaurants. We also give dinner parties at home once a month, which are organised by a caterer. I have driven my own BMW throughout the marriage. The Respondent has always expected me to dress well, and in recent years I have shopped principally at Marlene, a boutique in Weybridge where an outfit costs around £700.

Contributions

4.55   Question 4.3 asks about contributions. Detail here things like the contributions made to the purchase of a house or to investments, whether by a party or by his or her parents or other family member. An agreement by the parties that the wife would give up her job to bring up the children should be included here, as should involvement by the wife in her husband's career as a 'corporate wife'. Similarly, a husband's contribution to a wife's career should be made here. For example if he spent long evenings after work helping her to pass professional examinations, or made sacrifices in his own career, perhaps by being the parent who always ensured that he was home from the office to look after the children after school. This might be an entry for a wife who has 'not worked' during the marriage, but who has otherwise made an exceptional contribution:

4.3 Are there any particular contributions to the family property and assets or outgoings, or to family life, that have been made by you, your partner or anyone else that you think should be taken into account? If so, give a brief description of the contribution, the amount, when it was made and by whom.

When we first married, we rented a small flat in Islington. I became pregnant on our honeymoon, and we agreed that, as the Respondent had a good job, I would give up my career as a barrister to look after our family. Just before our daughter was born in 1989, my great Aunt died, leaving me £250,000. We purchased our first house, on the edge of Regent's Park, using this money, and took out a mortgage of £50,000 to renovate it. When our daughter was about three months old, I started to work on the house myself. I re-wired and re-plastered all the ground floor rooms, and papered and painted them. I made all the curtains and upholstered a good deal of our furniture, which I had inherited on the death of my grandmother in 1982. By

> *this time, the Respondent was in line for promotion and I devoted a great deal of time to entertaining his business contacts, organising dinner parties often three times a week until just before the birth of our twins in 1994. I continued to entertain once the twins were about four months old. On the death of my mother in 1996, after a long illness during which I had nursed her daily, I inherited £200,000. I invested this in a portfolio of shares in the joint names of the Respondent and me. I have made all the investment decisions in relation to this portfolio, which is currently worth about £750,000.*

Conduct

4.56 The issue of 'conduct' may be raised in reply to question 4.4. It can be even more difficult than in a narrative affidavit, to persuade a client that their spouse's boorish behaviour, which grounded a behaviour petition, has no relevance in financial proceedings and should be omitted. Concentrate their minds on exploring issues which would be relevant, like the dissipation of assets, or concealing income for other purposes, like drinking or gambling. 'Behaviour' is only likely to be relevant here if it is so bad that it made the spouse who suffered it ill, or otherwise unable to work, or less successful in their job than they would otherwise have been. It may be appropriate to mention here that a spouse was persuaded to dispose of an asset through coercion or deceit, if it is included, it may also be appropriate to refer to it at question 5.4, as a disposition which the client seeks to avoid.

Other circumstances

4.57 Question 4.5 asks for 'details of any other circumstances which could *significantly* affect the extent of the financial provision to be made…' [our italics]. The question itself lists the most common of these circumstances. One is earning capacity, which will include whether either party's earnings are likely to increase or decrease and why. Another is disability, either of one of the parties, or of a child or dependent, which may therefore impact both on the party's earning capacity and also perhaps on his or her income and capital requirements. Inheritance prospects are usually only of great significance where the inheritance is either very large, or likely to fall in very soon. Courts are increasingly chary of taking into account a modest potential inheritance from a frail aged relative who may need some years of residential or institutional care, and therefore use up in fees what would have been the inheritance. Contingent liabilities, things like guarantees which the client has given, perhaps in relation to a mortgage, should be included in this section.

Financial details of a new partner

4.58 On the prototype Form E, this section asked for the financial details 'of your current spouse'. This led to large numbers of people trying to second-guess in a small box the likely content of their husband or wife's Form E. What the Form now asks for, brief details of the income and assets of another partner, is what it actually meant all along. This question causes a lot of rancour. Not only do many clients object vociferously to divulging the financial affairs of their current partner ('it has *nothing* to do with him/her'), but the new partner can put up their own objections. By the same token, the client who feels that they have been deserted for this new partner can become almost obsessive about finding out as many details about that partner as they can, and start muttering darkly about production appointments, or even private detectives.

4.59   From the practitioner's point of view, the big problem is caused by the words 'so far as they are known to you'. If a client is under strict instructions from the new partner to divulge nothing, the simplest way to achieve this is to deny all knowledge of his or her financial affairs. It is certainly not unknown for a man who has remarried, and has a child by his new wife, and who has bought a house jointly with her, to deny flatly that he has any understanding of how her finances work. It appears to us that many judges are pusillanimous about this issue at the First Appointment. In the circumstances outlined above, where a party is clearly being economical with the truth, a direction to answer the question might be helpful. This, with an indication that a judge at an FDR is likely to draw inferences if a reasonable answer is not given, might go some way to producing an outline of the new partner's finances.

Part 5 Order Sought

What kind of Order

4.60   So asks question 5.1. It is frequently impossible, at the stage of compiling disclosure, to determine what orders a party will wish the court to make. In very short marriages, where there are no children and both parties are self-supporting, it may well be reasonable to look at a clean break. Where there are middle-aged parties and children in their teens, it may be impossible to ascertain whether there will be enough capital for a clean break. Requests for earmarking orders under the Pension Act should be included here if appropriate, as should orders for the transfer of property or share portfolios and motor cars. It is rare, in our experience, for specific chattels to be included in this section, but there seems to be no reason why they should not be if desired. If in doubt, keep the prospective orders broad, and fairly general; they can be refined as part of an offer at the FDR stage, once you have more information.

Detail any specific transfers, variations or dispositions with which you are asking the Court to deal

4.61   Questions 5.2, 5.3 and 5.4 ask for details, respectively, of properties and other assets to be transferred, any pre- or post-nuptial settlements which are to be varied and dispositions of assets which are to be avoided. Give as much detail as you can, as the easier it is for the other party and the judge to identify what you want and why, the more time will be saved. Some example replies are as follows:

5.2 If you are seeking a transfer or settlement of any property or other asset, you must identify the asset in question.

> *I ask the Court to transfer into my sole name the former matrimonial home, Dunrobin, Court Lane, Justice Green, West Midlands, registered at H.M. Land Registry under title number JG 198465X. I also ask the Court to transfer into my sole name the endowment policy number F1947757 with Principal Registry Assurance, currently held in the joint names of the Respondent and me. I also ask to the Court to transfer to me the Rover motor car, registration number SEK 51E, of which the Respondent is currently the registered keeper, together with its cherished number plate.*

5.3 If you are seeking a variation of a pre- or post nuptial settlement, you must identify the settlement, by whom it was made, its trustees and beneficiaries, and state why you allege it is a nuptial settlement.

> *I ask the Court to vary the terms of the trust established by the Respondent in 1985, after the birth of our second son, Christopher. The trust is called the Beresford Family (1985) Settlement, and the trustees are the Respondent's brother, Rupert Beresford, and his sister, Eleanor Greenblatt. The Respondent transferred into this trust the freehold of the then matrimonial home, Chaucer House, Cambridge which had been in his sole name. This trust should not be confused with the Beresford Family (1958) Settlement, which was established by the Respondent's grandfather.*

5.3 5.4** If you are seeking an avoidance of disposition order, you must identify the property to which the disposition relates and the person or body in whose favour the disposition is alleged to have been made.

> *I ask the Court to set aside the gift of a parcel of shares which the Respondent gifted to his secretary, Fiona Hotwell, on or around 10 October, 1999. I do not know the details of the shares in question, but I have appended to this form a copy of a letter sent by the Respondent to Ms Hotwell on that date explaining that he had transferred shares to her 'to keep them away from that bitch' and that she would be hearing from his brokers shortly. It is clear from this letter that the Respondent has made this disposition to defeat my claims. I have returned the original of the letter to Ms Hotwell.*

Presentation of Form E

4.62   Under the Pilot Scheme, very little accompanied Form E. There may have been a few additional pages, perhaps a schedule of estimated income requirements and some pension documentation. Rarely, though, was there much which could not be attached within the confines of a single cardboard corner. The Amended Rules depart radically from this practice. The new Form E with all its attachments will be barely less bulky than the average set of replies to questionnaire and list of documents requested. Note that the rubric on the front of the Form does not state that the documents must be *exhibited*. In the fourth paragraph of the instructions, it says that documents must be 'attached'. In the next paragraph it indicates which sections compel the production of documents which must 'accompany' the Statement. So, which is it to be? Attach, or accompany? As well as being exchanged, these Forms are to be filed at the court. Courts are not accustomed to having substantial quantities of documents other than as part of the Court Bundle for a final hearing. Is the Court likely to insist that the documents be *bound* to Form E, as if the whole thing were an enormous affidavit? Possibly.

4.63   Our view is that, for ease of use, the entire statement, including all the prescribed documents, should be presented in the smallest ring binder possible. This should preferably be of the kind which has a clamp attachment (as most lever arch files do) to keep the papers in place if the rings should spring apart. All the documents should be separated by tagged dividers, numbered and cross-referenced to Form E.

4.64   If the courts object (and they may) then we suggest sewing up one copy for *filing*, and nevertheless *exchanging* copies in the format above.

4.65   Finally, on the subject of presentation. If using ring binders for the court, don't forget a label for the spine, as well as a front sheet.

Exchanging Forms E

4.66   Rule 2.61B (1) provides unambiguously that '[b]oth parties must, at the same time, exchange with each other, and each file with the court, a statement in Form E...'. The clear intention is to ensure, so far as is possible, a 'level playing field' and avoid one party having the advantage over the other of replying to a case, rather than setting out his own stall. So, what to do when, 35 days before the First Appointment, your client's Form E is finalised, polished, and bristling with prescribed documents in a neat ring binder, and all is silence on the other side. After sending a certain amount of righteous indignation by facsimile, the shrewd practitioner will watch his back. Send your own client's Form E to court and file it, but in a sealed envelope marked 'not to be opened until the Applicant's/Respondent's Form E is filed, without leave of a judge'. This should prevent an unscrupulous practitioner for the other party sending down a plausible outdoor clerk and having your client's Form copied, checking out your client's case, and still filing their own Form E and exchanging it too early to give rise to complaints that there is insufficient time to take instructions.

4.67   For this has been the curious experience with the Pilot Scheme. Although the Rules state (as do the Amended Rules), that From E must be filed and exchanged 35 days before the First Appointment, the practice is far more honoured in the breach than in the observance, and judges seem to take very little cognisance of the fact.

4.68   ARAG in its ongoing discussions was mindful of the inordinate length of time it seems to take to produce a Form E. It was also mindful also of the fact that the additional disclosure now to be provided would require a longer period of analysis. It was finally mindful of the fact that, compared with the Pilot scheme, the time between filing of Form A and the First Appointment was to be increased by an average of two weeks. It therefore suggested that the time for exchanging and filing Forms E be reduced by a week to give more time for analysis and, it was hoped, the beginnings of negotiations. It was not to be. The 35 day period remains.

Procedure following the exchange of Forms E

4.69   Under the Pilot Scheme, the next step was very simple. Send off the other party's Form E to the client, and take instructions about further disclosure. However, the Amended Rules, by providing for a significant amount of disclosure to accompany the initial financial statement may well achieve the result that no further disclosure is needed, particularly in cases where finances are comparatively simple. If so, it may be possible to enter negotiations immediately, and even to have offer and acceptance before there is any need to take any further action under the Amended Rules. It could be argued that, by insisting on what might be described as 'standard disclosure', the Amended Rules have tried effectively to 'fast track' the simpler cases.

Dealing with information or documents which have been delayed

4.70   What, though, does the practitioner do if time is pressing, and certain documentation which he intended to attach to Form E has not been forthcoming? The Amended Rules state that *'[n]o disclosure or inspection of documents may be requested or given between the filing of the application for ancillary relief and the First Appointment, except – (a) copies sent with Form E or in accordance with paragraph (5)...* '

1   Rule 2.61B(6).

4.71   Rule (5) states that:
'Where a party was unavoidably prevented from sending any document required by Form E, that party must at the earliest opportunity: (a) serve copies of that document on the other party, and (b) file a copy of that document with the court, together with a statement explaining the failure to send it with Form E '[1]

1   Rule 2.61B(5).

4.72   It is clear that a prescribed document must be forwarded to the Court together with an explanation for the delay in its provision. But what about explanatory documents? This is what the Rules say:
'Form E must have attached to it: (a) any documents required by Form E; and (b) any other documents necessary to explain or clarify any of the information contained in Form E '[1]

1   Rule 2.61B(3).

4.73   So, it appears that only the documents which are *required* on the face of Form E have to be sent on to the Court and the other side with explanations. But how does the word 'must' in Rule (3) fit in? Let us take a case, for example, where there are complicated restrictions on share options. The party's employer says that the restrictions are being clarified, but they have not produced the clarification in time for it to accompany Form E. This information is necessary to explain the nature of the share options, and so, in the words of Rule (3) it *must* accompany Form E. However, it is not actually *required* by Form E. Presumably it is necessary to exchange and file it even if it is late, but equally it appears that no explanation to the court is needed when it *is* filed.

4.74   Even if the instructions on the front of Form E are a little unclear, common sense dictates that the document should be disclosed as soon as possible. The purpose of the rules limiting disclosure, as we understand it, is to prevent the running up of costs arguing about the extent of voluntary disclosure without the Court's intervention, and to avoid the parties having much more knowledge than the judge at the First Appointment/FDR. The parties are given a great deal of leeway under the Amended Rules about how much documentation they produce to accompany Form E. It would make a nonsense of the system if, having decided that a document is needed, delay by a third party in providing that document made it impossible to disclose before the First Appointment.

4.75   If a delay occurs, simply leave a gap for the document in the ring binder or, preferably, put in its place a sheet of paper which describes the document and says 'to follow', and then send it off when it arrives. Include with the copy to the court a brief note about the cause of the delay. Take a spare copy when going to court, as the chances of a loose document being married up with the file is, as all practitioners know, usually slim.

Further action before the First Appointment

4.76   *The following must be filed and served no later that 14 days before the First Appointment:*

1   a concise statement of the issues between the parties;
2   a chronology;
3   a questionnaire, setting out by reference to the concise statement of issues any further information and documents requested from the other party or a statement that no information and documents are required
4   a notice in Form G stating whether the party will be in a position at the First Appointment to proceed on that occasion to a FDR appointment;
5   confirmation that notice has been given, if appropriate, pursuant to Rules 2.59 (3) and (4) and Rule 2.70 (4)

4.77   Unless the case is clearly likely to settle very quickly, there should be no delay in dealing with these remaining steps once Forms E have been filed and exchanged.

4.78   It is possible, therefore, to divide cases from exchange of Form E until the First Appointment into two streams. First, there are those cases where no further disclosure is required. These cases may or may not settle, depending on what the issues between the parties are. If they can be settled before the First Appointment, then that appointment may be used to ask the court to consider making a consent order in the agreed terms. If settlement is not possible, then the case will be suitable for an immediate FDR appointment, and notice should be given to the court in Form G to that effect.

4.79   Although it comes late in the list, it is helpful to look next at Form G, as it will influence the remainder of preparation for the First Appointment.

Completing Form G where there is to be an FDR

4.80   Form G did not form part of the Pilot Scheme, and so it is not possible to give definitive instructions for its completion. Nevertheless, for a case where no further disclosure is required, the following is a suggested form of words:

> '... *the Applicant/Respondent will be in a position to proceed on that occasion with a Financial Dispute Resolution appointment for the following reasons:*
> *1   The Applicant considers that the Respondent has provided sufficient documentary disclosure;*
> *2   There are a number of issues, as set out in the Applicant's Statement of the Apparent issues, which it has not been possible to resolve, upon which the Applicant asks for the court's guidance.'*

The judge will make the decision where one party says that the First Appointment should be treated as an FDR, and the other says that it should not. It is not yet clear how individual judges will determine the question. However, one experienced District Judge in a non-Pilot Scheme court was recently heard to say, when this question was raised before him in a discussion: 'woe betide anyone who comes to my court and is not prepared to negotiate'. It is to be hoped that other judges take a similar stance. It would certainly be reasonable to agree to an FDR in Form G, while expressing reservations, because of a possibility that further disclosure may be required if certain concessions are not made at that appointment, for example:

> '... *the Applicant/Respondent will be in a position to proceed on that occasion with a Financial Dispute Resolution appointment for the following reasons:*

   1 The Applicant considers that the Respondent has provided sufficient
     documentary disclosure for an FDR appointment to take place;
   2 There are a number of issues, as set out in the Applicant's Statement of the
     Apparent issues, which it has not been possible to resolve, upon which the
     Applicant asks for the court's guidance.
   3 The Applicant has prepared a questionnaire and list of further documents
     requested and, in the event that this matter cannot be resolved at an initial FDR
     appointment, the Applicant will ask the court to order that those questions be
     answered and the documents provided by the Respondent.'

4.81 This approach would follow an increasing trend, which had been noticed at
First Appointments. That is to differentiate between questions (and particularly
documents) on a questionnaire and list of documents requested, which should be
answered or provided *before* an FDR, and those which need only be addressed if the
case fails to settle at or immediately after the FDR.

Completing Form G where there is to be no FDR

4.82 It is to be hoped that the cases where the First Appointment cannot be used, at
least in part, as an FDR will be in the minority. They are likely to be the more
complicated cases, where the prescribed documentation to accompany Form E is
simply insufficient to give a clear picture of a party's position. Of course, even in very
complicated cases, parties can chose to provide more documentation with the FDR
than merely the documents upon which the Rules insist. Other steps, too, may be taken.
If it is clear that the value of a particular property is going to be in issue, and there is
no recent valuation of it, why not at least put an estate agent's 'sale price' valuation
in place? To leave comparatively minor disclosure until a First Appointment because
no one has been bothered to deal with it will simply run up costs unnecessarily.

4.83 A response in Form G in a more complex case might be as follows:
   '... the Applicant/Respondent will not be in a position to proceed on that occasion
   with a Financial Dispute Resolution appointment for the following reasons:
   1 The Applicant considers that the Respondent has provided insufficient
     documentary disclosure for an FDR appointment to take place. The documents
     required are listed in full in the Applicant's Questionnaire and List of
     Documents requested;
   2 In particular, the Applicant considers that the question of whether or not a
     clean break is possible in this case is dependant upon the nature of the
     Respondent's interest in the Beresford Family (1985) Settlement, and upon
     any restrictions inhibiting his sale of shares in Tubthumpers Limited.'
See also page 46 below, which deals with the late filing and exchange of Forms E.

The remaining preparation

4.84 Under the Pilot Scheme Rules, the Questionnaire and the List of Documents
Requested were separate documents, and were to be filed and served just seven days
before the First Appointment, together with the Statement of the apparent Issues in the
case. (In fact the Questionnaire and List of Documents were frequently prepared as a
single document, and this fact has been recognised by the Amended Rules). However,
it cannot have escaped the attention of ARAG that many Pilot Scheme practitioners
treated the Concise Statement of the Apparent Issues as something to be jotted down
at the last minute once the Questionnaire had been prepared. It certainly did not appear
to be concentrating minds, as the progenitors of the Pilot Scheme intended.

4.85   The Amended Rules therefore state that the Questionnaire and List of Documents must be prepared with reference to the statement of issues: ie prepare the statement first.

The concise statement of issues

4.86   There is considerable debate about the most appropriate form for a concise statement of the issues in a case. Some practitioners favour a narrative style, or simply provide a list of issues. In our experience, the most helpful statement is set out along the lines of a Scott Schedule. Compare the following examples. First, the narrative:

'The Applicant wishes to remain in the matrimonial home, a four bedroom house worth about £350,000. The Respondent says that this is too large for her needs, and that she should move to a three bedroom house which would cost about £280,000. The Applicant considers that she needs maintenance for herself of £45,000 per annum, as stated in her Form E, but the Respondent believes that this is too high and that £35,000 is sufficient. The Applicant believes that she should retain all the furniture in the matrimonial home as it would be disturbing to the children for their surroundings to be changed dramatically, as would happen if the Respondent were to remove all the antique furniture, as he wishes to do';

4.87   Then the tabular schedule:

ISSUE	APPLICANT'S CASE	RESPONDENT'S CASE
Housing	A should remain in the FMH. She needs four bedrooms, and could not buy another suitable home for less than the £350,000 which the house is worth	A should sell the FMH and buy a three bedroom house, of the type illustrated in the particulars annexed to his Form E at divider 16. This would release about £70,000 for his housing needs.
Income	A needs £45,000 per annum for herself. Her needs are set out in her Form E, and cannot reasonably be reduced. The Respondent has access to all the income produced by the Beresford Family (1985) Settlement; this is a so-called *Brown v Brown* trust.	A needs no more than £35,000 for herself. Her budget is predicated on her remaining in the FMH, which is too large for her reasonable needs, and she has in any event exaggerated the costs of utilities, clothing, entertaining and holidays. In addition, the Respondent has been told by the trustees of the Beresford Family (1985) Settlement that they do not intend to make any further income available to him after this year
Chattels	A wishes to retain all the furniture in the FMH. The children have already been traumatised by the Respondent's departure, and their home should be left intact as far as possible. Much of the furniture was purchased jointly, contrary to what the Respondent says in his Form E	The Respondent should take the antique furniture in the FMH, which he inherited from his great aunt. The furniture is worth approximately £30,000 and, although there are one or two pieces which the Respondent hopes to retain for sentimental reasons, he will need to sell most of it to repay debts.

4.88 Our view, and it has found favour with the great majority of judges in our experience, is that the tabular schedule is to be preferred.

4.89 (It is not, though, universally the case. One practitioner who habitually adopted the tabular approach to schedules of issues ventured for one First Appointment many miles outside his familiar territory. He greeted with a barely concealed metropolitan sneer the other party's three line 'list' of issues, and went into court filled with the confidence that only the knowledge of superior preparation can achieve. The District Judge picked up his comprehensive and thorough schedule. She sniffed disapprovingly. 'I didn't expect a novel', she barked. Then her eye alighted fondly on the other schedule. She held it aloft. 'This is what they're supposed to look like', she explained).

The chronology

4.90 Everyone knows how to produce a chronology, but what are the Amended Rules trying to achieve by asking for one as part of the disclosure before a First Appointment? Judges operating the Pilot Scheme found that, although they had Forms E, there would often be nowhere a summary of the history of the marriage to give them a view at a glance of things like the length of the marriage, the ages of the parties and the children and the financial history of the marriage (like the parties' house and career moves). This was inevitable with the loss of the narrative affidavit.

4.91 Chronologies are an addition to the Pilot Scheme, and it will be interesting to see how practitioners approach them. As they may well be the judge's first contact with the case, it may be useful where there has been behaviour falling short of 'conduct', but which is nevertheless significant, to introduce this very briefly into the chronology, as in the following example:

Beresford – Chronology

DATE	EVENT
12.11.52	*Respondent born (47)*
15.06.55	*Applicant born (45)*
00.08.77	*Parties meet*
10.09.77	*Marriage*
12.12.77	*Parties purchase first matrimonial home , 3 beds in Esher for £60,000 (£10,000 deposit from A's inheritance)*
12.05.78	*Alice born (21)*
07.01.80	*R takes directorship of Tubthumpers, Limited.*
22.03.82	*Thomas born (18)*
00.07.84	*R starts affair with Fiona Hotwell*
06.09.84	*Rupert born (16)*
24.03.85	*Parties buy new home at Oatlands Ridge, Weybridge, for £190,000. Deposit of £50,000 from net proceeds of sale of Esher house.*
14.05.90	*R becomes managing director of Tubthumpers Limited*
31.07.91	*Fiona Hotwell gives birth to R's son, Damian*
00.09.91	*R starts affair with Tracy Hotwell, Fiona's sister*
24.12.93	*A in hospital for three days following violent argument with R about size of Christmas turkey*
15.03.96	*Emma born (4)*

12.11.97	*Parties separate. R goes to live with Fiona Hotwell*
10.10.99	*R transfers parcel of shares to Fiona Hotwell*
28.12.99	*A issues petition (2 years' separation)*
01.02.00	*Tracy Hotwell gives birth to R's daughter, Tiffany*
05.02.00	*Decree* Nisi
08.07.00	*A files Form A*

4.92   Of course, how much prejudicial material you decide to put in your chronology will be a highly tactical decision. It may be counter productive to antagonise the other party with a controversial chronology if negotiations are proceeding constructively. However, if you take the view that the behaviour cannot reasonably or appropriately be included in the Form in at either section 4.4 or 4.5, then the chronology is the only opportunity to give the judge the flavour of the case, unless the behaviour is spelt out clearly in the petition.

The questionnaire and list of documents requested

4.93   It would be fair to say that the majority of practitioners who operate under the Pilot Scheme have not adapted significantly their practice when drafting questionnaires from the techniques which they adopted for Rule 2.63 questionnaires under the FPR 1991. This begs the question of how such practitioners will fare under the Amended Rules. Everyone could manage to trot out at least a short questionnaire, if only to have a look at some bank and credit card statements and tax returns. But in how many cases now will questionnaires be relevant? The fact that the rules provide that a statement may be filed to say that no information and documents are required[1] suggests that this eventuality is anticipated in more than just a handful of cases. If the Amended Rules have been complied with, each party will have along with the Form E well in advance of the First Appointment the following documents:

1   A valuation of the matrimonial home and of any other properties if one has been obtained in the last six months;
2   The last twelve months' bank statements for all accounts listed;
3   Surrender value quotations of all life insurance policies;
4   The last two years' accounts of any business in which the other party has an interest;
5   His or her last three payslips, and P60 for the most recent year; and
6   The last two years' accounts for any self-employment, or any partnership of which he or she is a part.

There will also be valuations of pension rights if these are available.

1   Rule 2.61(B)(7)(c).

4.94   All of which reduces considerably the scope of a questionnaire. If the other party is being helpful, you may in addition have received a raft of further documentation, including calculations relating to CGT liability, explanations of restrictions on share dealing, details of trusts and valuations of business interests. The only documents which it appears unlikely that either side will provide with Form E is credit card statements. These will not always be relevant, but they are likely to come into issue where the payor (let us say the husband) is questioning his wife's budgeted expenditure, and she wishes to demonstrate that his own spending in the areas which he is challenging is greatly in excess of what she is claiming.

4.95   Assuming that the 'voluntary' discovery was not forthcoming with Form E, then a questionnaire must be drafted with reference to the Statement of Issues, which is a novelty for everyone. As an example, we have based the following questionnaires on the statement of issues at p 34:

Beresford – Applicant's Questionnaire and Request for Documents

1   *The Respondent states in his Form E that the trustees of the Beresford Family (1985) Settlement do not intend to make further payments of income to him from the end of the current year. Please provide a copy of the trust deed for this settlement, and copies of any correspondence between him and the trustees during the last three years, together with a schedule of all payments made to him from the trust during that period.*

2   *The Respondent always spent lavishly during our marriage on his numerous credit and charge cards on clothes, holidays, and entertaining, and I believe that he continues to do so. In the event that he intends to challenge my statement of my reasonable income needs, he should provide a schedule of all credit, charge and store cards held by him during the last twelve months, whether in his sole name, joint names or upon which he has signing rights, together with copy statements for all the accounts listed for the like period.*

3   *The Respondent states in his Form E that the antique furniture at the former matrimonial home was inherited by him on the death of his great aunt. He should provide a copy of the will of his great aunt, together will a copy of the inventory of the contents of her home made for probate purposes by Christies after her death in 1996.*

4.96   In *his* questionnaire, the Respondent might ask for copies of the Applicant's credit cards for the last twelve months to establish what her expenditure on the disputed items had actually been, and also for copies of any receipts for antiques which she claims had been purchased during the marriage.

Confirmation of service of copies of the application pursuant to Rule 2.59 (3) and (4) and Rule 2.70 (4), if applicable

4.97   Another new provision within the Amended Rules is that the applicant shall *confirm* that they have served the following with copies of Forms A and E[1] :

1   The trustees and settlor (if living) of any settlement in respect of which an application for variation has been made[2];
2   The person(s) to whom is alleged to have been made a disposition in respect of which an application for an avoidance of disposition has been made[3] ;

and the following with a copy of the Form A:

1   Any mortgagee of property in respect of which has been made an application for a property adjustment order[4] ;
2   The trustees or managers of any pension scheme in respect of which an application had been made which imposes upon those trustees or managers any requirements by virtue of the Matrimonial Causes Act 1973 sections 25B or 25C[5] , together with the other information required, namely:
     (a)   an address to which any notice which the trustees or managers are required to serve under the Divorce etc (Pensions) Regulations 1996 is to be sent;
     (b)   an address to which any payment which the trustees or managers are required to make to the applicant is to be sent; and

(c)   where the address in sub paragraph (b) is that of a bank, a building society or the Department of National Savings, sufficient details to enable payment to be made into the account of the applicant.

1   Rules 9(3) , (4)(*a*), (*b*).
2   Rule 2.59(3)(*a*).
3   Rule 2.59(3)(*b*).
4   Rule 2.59(4).
5   Rule 2.70(4).

4.98   There is no prescribed form for confirmation that the persons listed above have been served. It could presumably be done by filing copies of the letters giving the relevant notices.

Preparation of a costs estimate in Form H

4.99   At the First Appointment, and indeed at every appointment under the Amended Rules, each party must produce an estimate of his or her costs up to that point. There is debate about whether this Form H should include all costs relating to financial matters, or, as it states 'Ancillary relief solicitor's costs', it should simply record the costs since proceedings began, ie since the issue of Form A. In any event, it should not include any costs relating to divorce proceedings or to any Children Act proceedings.

4.100   On balance, we incline to the latter view. No doubt in due course one or other approach will be adopted by the courts: until that time it may be helpful for Forms H to be marked with the method chosen.

4.101   For example: '*The Respondent's costs of ancillary relief and financial matters from first consultation with Instructing Solicitors on 17 March, 2000 up to and including the First Appointment on 1 October, 2000*';
alternatively: '*The Respondent's ancillary relief costs from the issue of Form A on 14 July, 2000 up to and including the First Appointment on 1 October, 2000*'.

4.102   It is of note that Form H is *not* a Statement of Costs within the definition of that Statement in the Civil Procedure Rules 1998 (CPR 1998). Not only does it not specify the charge out rates of the fee earners involved in the case, it does not require certification that it does not breach the indemnity principle. It is not intended to be more than an estimate. Practitioners should be aware that, if costs fall to be assessed at a later date, it may be difficult to persuade an assessing officer that more costs should be recovered up to a particular point in the litigation if a lower sum appears on the costs estimate. It is reasonable to err on the side of caution for your client, therefore, when preparing the estimate.

4.103   If, as may be the case, an application is to be made for summary assessment at an appointment, for which see more below, then a Statement of Costs must be prepared in conjunction with the CPR 1998. In accordance with those Rules, this must be filed and served no less than 24 hours before the hearing.

4.104   There has been some surprise that judges have not reacted more strongly to some of the higher estimates which come before them at First Appointments. It can be disappointing, when one sees that the other party's costs are double or more than one's own, to have a judge merely remark to the court that already £X has been used up in fees. Judges usually then add words to the effect that as a rule of thumb, those costs will probably double between that point and the FDR.

4.105 *Very* occasionally, a judge may remark that such-and-such a firm's costs seem considerable. Presumably the judges work on the principle that as they cannot gauge how much work has been done on a party's behalf. Even in a simple case, they cannot know how much time the client may have taken up. It is, therefore, inappropriate for them to undermine a client's confidence in his or her legal team by criticising the level of fees.

CHAPTER 5 – THE FIRST APPOINTMENT

Attendance

5.01 Remember that both parties must attend the First Appointment unless the court orders otherwise[1]. This instruction appears in bold type on the front of the Form C, which both parties are likely to have seen. Practitioners will, before issuing Form A have checked their own and their clients' unavailable dates (and, obviously, those of counsel if the case is such that counsel are involved at this early stage).

1 Rule 2.61D(5).

5.02 Those acting for the Respondent to the application will have ensured that they and their clients can attend the First Appointment on the return date. If there is a serious difficulty in attendance, they will have made representations to the Applicant's solicitors and to the court to try to have the hearing re-listed, or to ask that the Respondent be excused from attending. This is a not infrequent application and may arise, for example, where the Respondent is a businessman with a very full schedule who cannot get to the First Appointment but does not wish the progress of the case to be delayed.

5.03 In our experience of the Pilot Scheme, courts have rarely made difficulty in releasing one or other party from attendance at the First Appointment if their problems in attending have been genuine. However it should be remembered that under the Pilot Scheme it would be almost unheard of to treat the First Appointment as an FDR. Under the Amended Rules there is a strong probability that through the representation of one or other of the parties or by the intervention of the judge of his or her own motion, at least some part of the First appointment will be treated as an FDR. Therefore the days of easy release for parties from attendance may be numbered.

5.04 Don't forget, then to remind the client well in advance that they must come to the First Appointment. This may be the first time that the clients have been in court in relation to their marriage. It may even be the first time your client has been in court in his or her life. However blasé practitioners may be about what many of them see as glorified directions appointments, they should make allowances for 'first time nerves'. Also, this may be the first time that the clients have seen each other for some time, and trepidation about the court process may be the last thing on their mind.

The judge's role

5.05 Rule 2.61D states that:
> 'The First Appointment must be conducted with the objective of defining the issues and saving costs'[1].

1 Rule 2.61D(1).

5.06   This dictum should, therefore, colour the judge's approach to the rest of his or her duties at the First Appointment.

5.07   There is no direction that the parties and their advisors should arrive in advance of the time of the First Appointment. If it has not been possible to agree about which questions should be answered and which documents produced before the day, though, it may be useful to suggest to the other parties advisors that the matter is raised at court just before the appointed time.

5.08   The format of First Appointments is likely to vary slightly from court to court. Technically it is for the Applicant to open. Like the system regulated by the FPR 1991 before amendment, applications are usually made by the potential recipient of awards, which is usually the wife. If the other party has made the application, perhaps from a keenness to take matters forward, then they may argue that they have the right to open. This is a misconception. In these circumstances it should be agreed between the parties that the 'true' applicant should open.

5.09   Openings at First Appointments under the Pilot Scheme have tended to be very short. Given that the Amended Rules provide the judge with a brace of chronologies, this tendency is unlikely to change.

5.10   It is to be presumed that if part of the First Appointment is to be treated as an FDR, it will be the earlier part. There seems little point in determining issues relating to further disclosure, and giving directions for a future FDR, if there is a realistic chance that the case may settle there and then. One difficulty with the conversion of First Appointments to FDRs is that of timetabling. The general experience of practitioners is that judges in courts operating the Pilot Scheme have been very flexible about their timetables, and allowed the parties very substantial amounts of time for negotiation. It is impossible to predict how the courts' listings departments will deal with cases where there is a full list of First Appointments on a day, and the majority indicate in Form G that they wish the appointment to be used as an FDR. We can only hope that flexibility will prevail, otherwise this laudable attempt to save costs is likely to be far less effective than it could.

5.11   If all or part of the First Appointment is to be treated as an FDR, presumably Rule 2.61E, which regulates FDRs, will apply. We shall deal with such appointments along with FDRs proper, below.

Dealing with the Questionnaires and Lists of Documents

5.12   Rule 2.61D (2) provides that:
  'At the First Appointment the district judge –
  (a)must determine –
      (i)   the extent to which any questions seeking information under rule 2.61B must be answered, and
      (ii)   what documents requested under rule 2.61B must be produced,
  and give directions for the production of such further documents as may be necessary.

5.13   Already under the Pilot Scheme we have seen a tendency on the part of judges to 'clamp down' on excessive questionnaires and lists of documents. In the early days of the Pilot Scheme there still existed a tendency to press a couple of keys on a word processor, generate the standard issue Rule 2.63 questionnaire and then tinker with it at the margins to adapt it to the case in hand. There is an illustrative story of the rather grand London firm which was in the habit of firing off a 'standard' questionnaire. Unfortunately their tinkering to fit it to one very modest case in hand was so marginal that they included a request to the other party, a minor civil servant to 'provide full details, including unladen weight, of all your capital ships'.

5.14   This story may be apocryphal. Nevertheless, many firms have been guilty of considerable thoughtlessness when seeking further disclosure. We have no doubt that judges will be assiduous in linking questions asked and documents requested to the matters which remain in issue.

5.15   If there is no argument about the wife's budget other than whether it can be sustained on the family's income, why does the husband necessarily need to produce his credit card statements? It is a different matter if the wife is alleging that he has a higher income than he has declared, but if this is the case, it should appear on the statement of issues.

5.16   If the wife wants more than a year's worth of bank statements, what is her reasoning? True, copy bank statements are cheap to obtain, but they are expensive to analyse. If there is a particular transaction, for example the sale of a property eighteen months earlier, which the wife thinks may have been dealt with through an undisclosed bank account, then the request is not unreasonable. But every request must relate to an issue and the issue must be both relevant and, most importantly, proportionate in the context of the case.

5.17   Sometimes, practitioners are put under considerable pressure by clients to ask for broader disclosure than they consider necessary. It is true that, while arguing a tendentious point on a Rule 2.63 questionnaire might involve an unnecessary outing to court and an adverse costs order if one failed in the request, under the Amended Rules, there has to be a First Appointment in any event. Nevertheless, the client should be warned that a lengthy battle for inappropriate disclosure may well result in an adverse costs order being made, especially if a judge takes the view that the possibility of using the First Appointment as an FDR has thereby been lost. This behaviour is not in the spirit of the Pilot Scheme or the Amended Rules, and it is to be hoped that practitioners will not encourage it.

5.18   If clients absolutely insist on unnecessary disclosure being sought, practitioners should make certain that their instructions are unequivocal, and be assiduous in giving (and recording the giving of) appropriate advice about relevance and proportionality. If they fail to do so, they may find difficulties in recovering costs not only on standard basis assessment, but even on the solicitor and client basis.

5.19   One final point is that the judge, in his role as an active manager of the case[1] may make an order requiring additional disclosure to that requested by either of the parties if he thinks that it is necessary for the disposal of the case.

1   Rule 2.51B(5).

5.20   Having disposed of the questionnaires, the judge turns again to Rule 2.61D(2) which instructs him that he:

'(b) must give directions about –
- (i) the valuation of assets (including, where appropriate, the joint instruction of joint experts);
- (ii) obtaining and exchanging expert evidence, if required; and
- (iii) evidence to be adduced by each party and, where appropriate, about further chronologies or schedules to be filed by each party.

5.21   As far as (i) and (ii) are concerned, Rule 2.61C provides that:
'CPR rules 35.1 to 35.14 relating to expert evidence (with appropriate modifications), except CPR rules 35.5(2) and 35.8(4)(*b*), apply to all ancillary relief proceedings.

5.22   During the lengthy discussions leading to the final formulation of the Amended Rules, many commentators envisaged that the Civil Procedure Rules on expert evidence would be incorporated within the Family Proceedings Rules as part of the amendment. This did not happen for, apparently, three reasons. First, any amendment to the CPR would entail further amendment to the Family Proceedings Rules; secondly, the incorporation of a large part of the CPR into the middle of the Family Proceedings Rules would unbalance those rules (and thereby perhaps cause confusion to family lawyers?). Thirdly, and possibly most importantly, there is a lingering question mark over the *vires* of part of the CPR rules on expert evidence, which might cause additional complications if repeated in a different set of rules.

5.23   The CPR Rules are reproduced at Appendix C. We summarise them as follows:
1   There is a duty to restrict Expert evidence to that which is reasonably required to resolve the proceedings[1].

2   Experts have an overriding duty to the court, which overrides any obligation to the party who is instructing them, or to the person who pays them[2].

3   Neither party may call an expert or put in evidence an expert's report without the court's permission; he must identify the field in which he requires expert evidence, and if possible, an appropriate expert. Permission from the court will be limited to the field/expert in question, and the court may limit the amount of fees which may be recovered in any event from the other party[3].

4   Expert evidence must be in the form of a written report[4].

5   The party who has not instructed the expert witness may, on one occasion, put written questions to the expert having seen his report, for the purpose of clarification, and the answers to those questions will be treated as part of the expert's report. If he does not answer such a question or questions, the court may disallow the evidence of the expert and/or prevent the instructing party from recovering the expert's costs from the other party[5].

6   Where two parties wish to submit expert evidence on a particular issue, the court may direct that the evidence on that issue is to be given by one expert only, and may direct the manner in which the expert is to be selected, if this cannot be agreed. It may also make directions in relation to what the expert may do in order to enable him to make his report, and how he is to be paid[6].
7   The court may direct a party which has information not accessible to the other to provide information to that other party[7].

8   An experts report must comply with the specific standards set out in the CPR Rules at Rule 35.10.

9   Any party may use a disclosed experts report as evidence, conversely, if the report is not disclosed, it may not be relied upon without the court's permission[8].

10   The court may, at any stage, direct a discussion between experts for the purpose of requiring the experts to identify the issues between them and, where possible, reach an agreement on an issue[9].

11   The expert may ask the court for directions as to how to carry out his function without giving notice to any party[10].

12   The court may appoint its own expert ('assessor') under section 70 of the Supreme Court Act 1981[11].

1   CPR rule 35.1.
2   CPR rule 35.3.
3   CPR rule 35.4(1).
4   CPR rule 35.5(1) (Rule 35.5(2) does not apply to ancillary relief cases).
5   CPR rule 35.6.
6   CPR rule 35.7 and 8 (Rule 35.8(4)(b) does not apply to ancillary relief cases).
7   CPR rule 35.9.
8   CPR rule 35.11 and 13.
9   CPR rule 35.12.
10 CPR rule 35.14.
11 CPR rule 35.15.

5.24   Experience with the Pilot Scheme suggests that judges will be disinclined at First Appointments to give orders for expert evidence unless absolutely necessary. There is considerable anecdotal evidence that the view taken in respect of property valuations is that an estate agent's 'selling price' valuation will suffice 'for the purposes of an FDR'. This is particularly true in metropolitan areas, which have large stocks of similar housing. It may raise problems in a case involving a remote and unusual property which has not been marketed for some years.

5.25   As for private companies and partnerships, often the value is only particularly relevant if they are to be sold, floated on the stock market, or if they have very high asset values. Directions for expert evidence in relation to such companies are more likely to be given at the end of an FDR.

5.26   As for further evidence, chronologies or schedules, further to 2.61D(b)(iii), these again are comparatively unusual at the First Appointment. They are likely to arise only if the parties or the judge identify a particular problem which the judge envisages will be a sticking point at the FDR. For example, there may be an argument about the prognosis of the health of a party (usually in the context of earning capacity), and a medical report or reports may be ordered. Similarly, there may be brewing a battle royal over chattels, and the judge may consider that a Scott Schedule will give the judge at an FDR a starting point from which to direct negotiations.

5.27   Rule 21D(2)(c) says that the judge:
   'must, unless he decides that a referral is not appropriate in the circumstances, direct that the case be referred to a FDR appointment'

5.28   Rule 21D(2)(d) gives him his choices of action if he decides that there should be no FDR. In such cases he must:

'…direct one of the following:

(i)   that a further directions appointment be fixed;

(ii) that an appointment be fixed for the making of an interim order;

(iii) that the case be fixed for final hearing and, where that direction is given, the district judge must determine the judicial level at which the case should be heard; or

(iv) that the case be adjourned for out-of court mediation or private negotiation or, in exceptional circumstances, generally'.

Fixing the FDR

5.29   In the vast majority of cases, the judge will fix an FDR. In the early days of the Pilot scheme, attempts were frequently made at First Appointments where the parties were a very long way apart, and negotiations were either stalled or had never really started, to 'skip' the FDR on the grounds that it would be a waste of time. Judges quickly took the view that such attempts to 'opt out' of the scheme should be discouraged and that FDRs were designed precisely for the purpose of attempting to dig out the entrenched, and bring them into negotiation.

5.30   Be warned that judges have widely differing views about the practicalities of listing FDRs. Some accept that the appointment should be fixed convenient to counsel who have been involved from the inception of the case. Others take a more robust line, which may make life difficult if the client has had a particularly successful conference with counsel and has expressed his or her confidence in them. Practitioners will rapidly get the measure of the attitudes of the judges in their 'home' courts. Given the problems with counsels' diaries generally, many practitioners find it a sensible precaution to advise clients that continuity of counsel is not always possible. This appears to be particularly true between the First Appointment and an FDR or other appointment.

Fixing a further directions appointment

5.31   A further directions appointment might be ordered where, for example, one party has failed to complete a Form E satisfactorily, or has failed to provide with it the prescribed documents. At the other end of the spectrum, it may be clear to the judge that the parties are so close to an agreement that to list an FDR would be using a sledgehammer to crack a nut. In such circumstances, he is more likely to list for directions, and suggest to the lawyers that if an agreement is reached in the next few days, they ask the court for a mention only, and vacate the further directions appointment.

Fixing an appointment for the making of an interim order

5.32   It is difficult to conceive of a case where a judge would not list an FDR just because he was listing an appointment for the making of an interim order. If he does though, then the hearing of the application for an interim order becomes an integral part of the new procedure. This means that the judge hearing that application must not only make an order on that application, but also make an order giving directions about the main ancillary relief application. He can do whatever a judge at a First Appointment could do: ie, fix an FDR or further directions appointment, a final hearing, adjourn for mediation, negotiation or generally in an exceptional case, or fix a further appointment for the making of another interim order.

Fixing a final hearing

5.33 The most likely eventuality in which this will occur is likely to be where all or part of the First Appointment has been used as an FDR, and it has proved completely abortive. It is perfectly possible to conceive of a case where the discovery in Forms E and the accompanying documents is sufficient to enable informed negotiations to take place, but the parties are simply too far apart to reach an agreement. It is also possible that the judge could consider that the issues are so complex, and the amount of expert evidence which must be obtained, weighed and sifted makes the case wholly inappropriate for an FDR. We envisage that such a case would probably have been started off in the High Court in any event; if not, the First Appointment would be an appropriate time to transfer it up. Note that, in any event, if he decides that a case should go straight from First Appointment to final hearing, the judge must, as part of that process, decide the appropriate judicial level for the final hearing.

Adjourning for out of court mediation, private negotiation or generally

5.34 It appears to us that these provisions are likely to be little used. The rules say that the judge may make *one* of the orders in Rule 2.61D(2)(d). therefore if he adjourns for one of these reasons, he cannot in addition fix a further appointment for directions and therefore the case is likely to drift. More likely course would be to list further directions at a longer time hence than might normally be the case, to give time for out of court mediation or private negotiation. As for adjourning generally, the only occasions where we can envisage the provision being used is where one party is seriously ill, and it is impossible to predict when, or if, they will recover, or if there is a jurisdiction dispute.

Costs of the First Appointment

5.35 Rule 2.61D(2)(e) provides that at the end of the First Appointment the judge:
  'must consider whether, having regard to all the circumstances (including the extent to which each party has complied with this Part, and in particular the requirement to send documents with Form E), to make an order about the costs of the hearing…'

5.36 There can be no clearer warning to the parties than this, that inadequate disclosure will not be tolerated. This is a warning which, in our view should be brought to the attention of all clients as early (and loudly) as possible. After issue of Form A there will be a minimum of seven and a maximum of nine weeks in which to complete the Form E and gather the documents which must be attached to it. As many Pilot Scheme practitioners have found to their cost, it is easy to be lulled into a false sense of security. Two months, or thereabouts, seems a long time. Don't delay. If your client is efficient and reliable, ask him to obtain the relevant documents, and chase him frequently in writing until they arrive. If his is less well organised, arm yourself with plenty of letters of authority from him and do the job yourself.

application be made if a new reason for needing the document or the reply emerged.

1   Chambers Twentieth Century Dictionary, p 435.

6.03   There seems, though, to be no prohibition on the *voluntary* exchange of relevant documentation or information. An example is as follows:

6.04   Immediately following the First Appointment, the Respondent is headhunted, and changes jobs. His solicitors, having reminded him of his duty of full and frank disclosure, write to the Applicant's solicitors and inform them of the change, and of his new salary and benefits. The Applicant's solicitors reply with a request for a copy of the Respondent's new contract of employment. They are not*entitled* to a copy; only a court order can entitle them. There is, though, nothing to stop them asking for it. The Respondent's solicitors can then take a view about whether this document is relevant, and whether they consider that the court would order them to produce it. If they decide not to produce it, then the Applicant may make an application in the usual way.

6.05   Similarly, the Applicant may realise that she has overlooked a bank account when completing her Form E. She has a duty of full and frank disclosure, and so the Respondent's solicitors are informed. Rule 2.61D(3) implies that the Respondent may not be *entitled* to receive copies of twelve months' statements for that account. However it seems axiomatic, given the requirements of Form E, that were he to make an application to the court for them, not only would the court order the discovery (or entitle him to receive the copies) but would also make a costs order against the Applicant if she resisted the application.

6.06   The 'bottom line' is that if there is a relevant document with either party then its *existence* must be *disclosed*. The parties can then argue about its *discovery* (or 'physical disclosure', if the term is preferred) in the usual way, with the usual costs implications.

Compliance with all directions made at the First Appointment

6.07   This goes without saying. If a party has failed to provide documents or supply replies to questionnaire, or does so out of time then he may jeopardise the effectiveness of the FDR and be at risk on costs. Of course, any *Calderbank* offer which he makes without having provided full disclosure will not protect him on costs. If there is a problem with disclosure for a good reason, either sort it out by consent with the other party, or return to court for further directions.

Filing of offers

6.08   Rule 2.61E(3) provides that:
   'Not later than seven days before the FDR, the Applicant must file with the court details of all offers and proposals, and responses to them.'

6.09   Rule 2.61E(4) explains that:
   'Paragraph (3) includes any offers, proposals or responses made wholly or partly without prejudice, but paragraph (3) does not make any material admissible as

evidence if, but for that paragraph, it would not be admissible.'

6.10 Therefore everything must go in. Even if the parties or their advisors have had without prejudice face to face or telephone discussions in which offers have been made, these must be summarised and filed.

Filing of costs estimates in Form H

6.11 These estimates must be produced as they were for the First Appointment (indeed, the swiftest and most cost-effective practice will probably be simply to update the last Form H). Again, if a party wishes to ask for the costs of the FDR because the other party has prevented it from being effective, he should file and serve a 'Woolf' Statement of Costs no later than 24 hours before the FDR.

Decree nisi

6.12 Both parties should be aware that an FDR may not be effective without decree *nisi* or a decree of judicial separation. The judge will be irritated if the decree is not in place unless there is good reason for the delay, as he will not be able to make a final order if agreement is reached. In extreme cases, he may even refuse to conduct the FDR at all, and simply treat the appointment as a directions hearing. In such circumstances, he may refuse to certify the matter fit for counsel, and there may be problems for both parties' solicitors in recovering costs from their clients for time thrown away. Keep an eye on decree *nisi*. It may be possible to apply to the court for it to be expedited in advance of the FDR if the is a reasonable explanation for the delay.

CHAPTER 7 – THE FDR

The purpose of the FDR

7.01 Rule 2.61E(1) states that:
    'The FDR appointment must be treated as a meeting held for the purposes of discussion and negotiation…'

7.02 This represents a change from the equivalent provision at Rule 2.75(1) under the Pilot Scheme, which provided that:
    'The FDR appointment shall be treated as a meeting held for the purposes of conciliation…'

7.03 Is this a significant change? If one regards 'conciliation' as a term encompassing the notion of without prejudice discussions, then it is. It is true that there is nothing about the phrase 'discussion and negotiation' which carries 'without prejudice' connotation but FDR appointments under the Pilot Scheme have always been treated as being without prejudice. It appears from the provisions in Rule 2.61E that this remains the intention. However, it may be as well to ask the judge at the beginning of the appointment for a specific direction as part of the order that all negotiations and discussions which will take place are to be treated as being without prejudice. Without this, it may be difficult to argue for the exclusion of references to the FDR in future *Calderbank* or even open correspondence. It is to be hoped that such a direction will swiftly become standard. It can surely not have been the draftsmens' intention, given the success of the Pilot Scheme FDRs, to reduce their effectiveness by making them prejudicial.

The format of the FDR

7.04   Like that of the First Appointment, the precise format of the FDR is likely to vary between courts, and even between judges within courts. Early in the Pilot Scheme, a number of judges pioneered some remarkably informal approaches to conducting the appointments. This even included in the more radical courts the novelty of all the participants, including the judge, sitting without distinction in the body of the court, and having, in effect, a round table meeting chaired by the judge. This approach rapidly fell out of favour, however, and Pilot Scheme judges for the most part have reverted to a more magisterial role.

7.05   One problem for the practitioner is that it can be difficult to predict how the judge will approach the appointment. Some judges will be heavily interventionist, and make their view very clear having read only the papers (and possibly skeleton arguments if these have been lodged). Others will listen courteously to the opening submission of the applicant and to the response, before opining that it really is a great pity that the parties cannot get closer, and that without agreement, costs are going to rise.

7.06   It is, therefore, impossible to be didactic about the shape of an FDR. It will *probably*, though, run something like this:

Step 1

7.07   *The parties arrive with their solicitors (and counsel if instructed) about an hour before the time listed on the Form D notice of an FDR.* (There seems, interestingly, to be no provision within the Rules for the service of Form D. The rules say that the judge will decide at that appointment whether an FDR will take place. The Rules do not, though, prohibit a judge making this decision in advance of the First Appointment. If this happens, presumably the Form D will be sent out once the decision has been made. Otherwise, we anticipate that it will accompany the order made at the First Appointment when it is sent out from the court. A Practice Direction about how practitioners will know in advance that a First Appointment is to be treated as an FDR would be appreciated)*. During this waiting period they will exchange skeleton arguments if such have been prepared, and attempt to narrow the issues between them still further from the position reflected in their respective statements of issues.*

Step 2

7.08   *The parties will be called into court.* If they are very close to an agreement, it may be appropriate to ask the judge for further time for discussion. Whether that time is forthcoming will depend very much on the individual judge. Some encourage further negotiation at this stage, others prefer to hear what the current position is in any event and give guidance. At some point, though, unless agreement is reached, will come

Step 3

7.09 *The commencement of the hearing.* As with the First Appointment, if the payer has made the application, it should be agreed that the payee, as the 'true' applicant, should open. The length of opening may depend on the presence or not of skeleton arguments, and whether the judge wishes to be taken through them at length. Remember that, unlike the practice under the Pilot Scheme rules, the judge will have chronologies from each party. Once the opening submission is complete, the response will be put. The atmosphere, although recognisably a hearing, is frequently comparatively relaxed, and the judge may well interrupt both submissions extensively to ask for clarification, or even to give an early indication of his or her opinion.

Step 4

7.10 *Discussions in the courtroom* follow. There may well be a good deal of discussion, usually between the judge and the solicitors (and counsel), although it is not unheard of for judges to bring the parties into the discussion, so warn the client that this is a possibility. This is not, though, a forum for the gathering or testing of evidence, and so neither party will be examined on oath. There is usually a good deal of give and take, and the appointment at this stage is frequently conducted more like a (civilised) debate than a formal hearing. Once each party's case has been aired, and the judge has given his indication, he may well invite the parties to go outside for

Step 5

7.11 *Continuation of negotiations.* This can take some time. Frequently the judge will invite the parties to carry on talking while he hears his next case, and invites the parties to return thereafter. If progress is being made, the judge may be content to be updated, and allow the parties further time. At some point before the court day ends, the judge will 'call time' and the parties will return to the courtroom for

Step 6

7.12 *A final order or further directions.* The nature of these will depend entirely on the extent to which progress has been made. If an agreement has been reached and a consent order drafted, the judge may, if he approves the agreement, make the order without further delay. If a *Xydias*[1] agreement has been reached, and only drafting points are preventing the making of an order, the judge may list for a mention. If considerable progress has been made he may adjourn the FDR, or list a second FDR. Certainly if progress has been made, judges operating the Pilot Scheme have generally been reluctant to list cases immediately for final hearing at the end of the FDR. They have been more inclined to fix a directions appointment for as close a date as possible, and indicate that directions for trial should be given at that appointment should no further progress have been made. Only if there has been little or no progress, and the parties are still polarised, will the judge give

1   Xydias v Xydias [1999] 1 FLR 683.

Step 7

7.13 *Directions for trial.* In so doing, he may give directions in respect of expert evidence which was not deemed appropriate at First Appointment, and in respect of the filing of other evidence. It is worth bearing in mind the dictum of Wilson J, recently reported as a fragment of the case of *W v W* (**Ancillary relief: Practice) Times (2000) 15 March,** His Lordship's view, as reported, was that:

> 'for the purpose of the financial dispute resolution scheme, historical background evidence in ancillary relief cases was rightly and necessarily limited. However, where upon failure of the dispute resolution the parties proceeded to a substantive hearing it was desirable, at any rate in cases of greater wealth, for the evidence to be broadened so that the court could perform its duty under section 25 of the 1973 Act. It would therefore often be helpful for directions to be given for narrative affidavits to be filed by each party which would, inter alia, illumine their respective contributions, the genesis of current resources and the standard of living during the marriage,'

7.14　Having given directions, as he is required to do[1], the judge will then proceed to Step 8.

1　Rule 2.61E(8).

Step 8

7.15　Return the documents detailing the offers, and any further filed documents which refer to them[1] (for example chronologies which contain the dates on which Calderbank offers were made). The wording of 2.61E(8) is curious. Whereas the equivalent provision in the Pilot Scheme rules provided that:

> '…at the conclusion of the appointment, any documents containing the same or referring thereto shall be returned to the applicant or the respondent (as the case may be) and not retained on the court file'[2],

the replacement rule states that:

> 'At the conclusion of the FDR appointment, any documents filed under paragraph (3), and any filed documents referring to them must, at the request of the party who filed them, be returned to him and not retained on the court file.'

1　Rule 2.61E(5).
2　Rule 2.75(1)(b).

7.16　The rules do not descend to the particulars of what happens to these documents if the party filing them does not request their return. Is the court obliged to retain them on the file? If so, where does this leave the principle that the FDR is without prejudice? The best advice appears to be: don't forget to ask for the return of the documents!

7.17　Remember that the judge who hears the FDR is not permitted to have any further involvement in the case, save to conduct further FDRs, and to make a consent order or a further directions order[1].

1　Rule 2.61E(2).

Some FDR dos and don'ts

1　**DO** make absolutely sure that your client appreciates that he or she has to attend the appointment[1]. It is possible that some clients may not have attended the First Appointment, so ensure that they are clear about how to get to the court. This is very obvious but, unlike most hearings other than a trial, this one cannot go ahead if there is any misunderstanding and the client does not arrive. Also, remember to ensure that the client arrives before the time of the FDR if there is a direction to do so, or if this has been agreed with the other side.

2   **DO** tell your client that although the appointment is only listed for an hour or two hours as the case may be, it could last all day. Point out that some judges are prepared to sit after the court closes at 4.30 if an agreement seems to be in sight. There are few more embarrassing things to have to tell a judge than that your client has to leave in the middle of negotiations to collect the children from school.

3   **DO** try to give your client as clear a picture as possible of what the format will be. This will become easier as the practitioners and local courts develop their own styles of approaching these appointments. Clients are likely to be very nervous, and they may have very major decisions to make. In this respect the FDR is unlike any other court appointment.

4   **DO** agree a 'bottom line' before the FDR that the client is prepared to accept, if you can do so. It may not be possible, but it will give the client a feeling of security if it is there.

5   **DON'T** then lose sight of the bottom line in the heat of the negotiations. Even if the judge is against you, remember, and remind your client, that an order cannot be made without the client's consent at this appointment. If the judge has thrown up a point which forces you to reconsider your approach to the case (and it can happen), you may be better to think it through in the days following the appointment than to change your stance and try to persuade the client to approve a consent order which he had not hitherto contemplated.

6   **DON'T** forget that the client may have 'lost the plot' if the appointment lasts all day, or if they were extremely nervous or worried before it even started. There can often be a great deal of pressure on clients at FDRs. It is tempting if the other party's offer looks good, is commended by the judge, and you are afraid that it may be withdrawn if they have time for reflection, to lean on the client to accept. There is a fine line between advising a client firmly and forcing instructions out of them.

7   **DO** let your client know *in writing* what the current offer is if the FDR is adjourned for only a short time. If they have misunderstood, now is the time to find out. One practitioner followed this rule when a an FDR was adjourned overnight, the judge having offered to sit early the following morning to try to help to resolve the final sticking point. Having received the letter by courier on the evening of the FDR, the client (who had been nodding his consent throughout the appointment) arrived the following morning and made it clear that he had not understood the offer, and did not agree with it. Thus on arrival for the resumed FDR, his solicitor was not only unable to make progress on the remaining outstanding point, but was obliged to resile from what had been tendered as the client's position the day before.

8   **DO** remind the client that he or she is required by the court to use his or her best endeavours to settle the case[2]. It is in the judge's power to make a punitive cost order if one party wilfully refuses to take part in the negotiations.

1   Rule 2.61E(9).
2   Rule 2.61E(6).

CHAPTER 8 – PREPARATION FOR THE FINAL HEARING

8.01   Preparation for trial under the Amended Rules is unchanged from the methods which prevailed under the Family Proceedings Rules 1991 save in these respects:

1   Rule 2.69E(1) provides that not less than 14 days before the date fixed for the final hearing of an application for ancillary relief, the applicant must (unless the court directs otherwise) file with the court and serve on the Respondent an open statement which sets out concise details, including the amounts involved, of any orders which he proposed to ask the court to make.

2   Rule 2.69E(2) provides that not more than 7 days after the service of a statement under paragraph (1), the Respondent must file with the court and serve on the applicant an open statement which sets out concise details, including the amounts involved, of the orders which he proposes to ask the court to make.

3   A costs estimate in Form H must be produced for the final hearing, as it must for any further directions hearing or additional or adjourned FDR which comes before the final hearing. (In fact, if the parties are very close to settlement at an FDR, and the judge lists for a mention only, it is customary to ask for a direction that preparation of a costs estimate be dispensed with at that mention, and judges will frequently make such a direction).

4   A careful stock must be taken in relation to *Calderbank* offers, as their effect on the incidence of costs has now altered considerably

8.02   The final hearing or trial is conducted exactly as under the old rules, as it was under the Pilot Scheme. The difference comes at the end of the hearing, after the judgment, when the issue of costs falls to be determined and here the rules have made some fundamental changes.

Chapter 9 – COSTS AFTER JUDGMENT AT THE FINAL HEARING

9.01   Under the Family Proceedings Rules, 1991, Rule 2.69 provided for the insertion of CCR Order 11, rule 10 (written offers 'without prejudice save as to costs') into the rules.

9.02   Rule 2.69 has now been substituted by a replacement of the same number. The first part of the new rule simply explains the *Calderbank* concept: 2.69(1) states that:
'Either party to the application may at any time make a written offer to the other party which is expressed to be 'without prejudice save as to costs' and which relates to any issue in the proceedings relating to the application'.

9.03   2.69(2) continues:
'Where an offer is made under paragraph (1), the fact that such an offer has been made shall not be communicated to the court, except in accordance with rule 2.61E(3) [at the FDR], until the question of costs falls to be decided'.

So far, so good. Now come the complicated bits.

Where the judgment or order is more advantageous than an offer made by the other party

9.04   Rule 2.69B is stated thus:

(1)   This rule applies where the judgment or order in favour of the applicant or the respondent is more advantageous to him than an offer made under rule 2.69(1) by the other party.

(2)   The court must, unless it considers it unjust to do so, order that other party to pay any costs incurred after a date beginning 28 days after the offer was made.

9.05   At first sight, this looks reasonable enough. Look at an example. A *Calderbank* offer is made by the husband. The wife does not respond. When the judgment is given, the wife does better than the husband's offer. Therefore unless the court considers it unjust to do so, the husband must pay any costs incurred by the wife from the date 28 days after the offer was made.

9.06   But where is the *quid pro quo*? What if the judgment is *less* favourable to the wife than the husband's *Calderbank*? Why should she not pay the *husband's* costs incurred from the date 28 days after he made the offer, unless the court considers it unjust for her to do so?

9.07   Presumably the court retains the *discretion* to order the wife to pay those costs, and would, in accordance with established jurisprudence, do so. It is inconceivable that the draftsman intended to abrogate years of established principle, and to give the wife an unfair advantage if she stays silent. This anomaly could be remedied by the removal of the words '…by the other party' at the end of Rule 2.69B(1).

Where the judgment or order is more advantageous than offers made by both parties

9.08   Rule 2.69C states:

'(1)   This rule applies where

    (a)   both the applicant and the respondent have made offers under rule 2.69(1);

    and

    (b)   the judgment or order in favour of the applicant or the respondent, as the case may be, is more advantageous to him than both of the offers referred to in paragraph (a).

(2)   The court may, where it considers it just, order interest in accordance with paragraph (3) on the whole or part of any sum of money (excluding interest and periodical payments) to be awarded to the applicant or the respondent, as the case may be.'

9.9   The Rule further provides that the rate of interest may not exceed 10% above base rate, and that the interest may run for some or all of the period beginning 28 days after the making of the offer[1]. The Court may also award indemnity costs in these circumstances, again in respect of the period commencing 28 days after the offer was made, and interest on those costs, again at a rate not exceeding 10% above base rate[2].

1   Rule 2.69C(3).
2   Rule 2.69C(4)(a) and (b).

9.10   The drafting of this Rule has created a great deal of controversy, and has generated some heated correspondence in legal journals. One school of thought suggests that a wife who is made a Rule 2.69(1) (*Calderbank*) offer by her husband, is better not to respond at all. She can fulfil her obligation to negotiate by making, or responding to, an open offer - indeed, a duty to do the latter at least 7 days before the final hearing is imposed upon her[1] – but should keep silent on a *Calderbank* basis. The rationale? Simply this: if she responds, and then the judgment goes against her and she fails to beat either her own or her husband's costs, then the court must[2] order her to pay her husband's costs, perhaps on an indemnity basis, and perhaps with interest. On the other hand, if she makes no *Calderbank* proposal, then although the court has the discretion to make her pay her husband's costs, there is no *obligation* on it to do so. The critics argue that, by allowing a wife to make a counter-*Calderbank* offer in these circumstances, practitioners may be exposing themselves to a later action for negligence.

1   Rule 2.69E(2).
2   But see below.

9.11   However, there is a corollary to this argument. True, if the wife makes no counter-*Calderbank* she runs no risk of the mandatory costs penalties imposed by Rule 2.69(C)(4), but equally, she has no prospect of having interest awarded on any lump sum which the court orders her husband to pay to her. There is an element here of 'gambling', but this is not new. What practitioners should certainly be scrupulous to do is to explain very carefully to their clients the costs implications of making, or not making a counter-*Calderbank* offer.

9.12   Practitioners should be wary of setting all their store by the new costs provisions. The 'word on the street' seems to be that Judges are not about to throw over all the old case law on the interaction of costs and negotiation. *Gojkovic*[56] remains!

9.13   One thing is clear, if the Lord Chancellor wished to make as certain as possible that *Calderbank* offers prompt a response, his draftsmen should, as we have pointed out, have omitted the words '…by the other party' at the end of Rule 2.69B(1).

Costs justice

9.14   Of course, everything which we have written in relation to Rules 2.69B and 2.69C must be read in the light of Rule 2.69D. It is this Rule which enables the court to determine whether it would be 'unjust' under Rule 2.69B or 'just' under Rule 2.69C, to make an order for costs in the terms of those rules.

9.15   Rule 2.69D states:
> '(1)   in considering whether it would be unjust, or whether it would be just, to make the orders referred to in rules 2.69B and 2.69C, the court must take into account all the circumstances of the case, including –
> (a)   the terms of any offers made under rule 2.69(1);
> (b)   the stage in the proceedings when any offer was made;
> (c)   the information available to the parties at the time when the offer was made;
> (d)   the conduct of the parties with regard to the giving or refusing to

give information for the purposes of enabling the offer to be
made or evaluated; and
(e)   the respective means of the parties.

(2)   The power of the court to award interest under rule 2.69C(2) and (4)(b)
        is in addition to any other power it may have to award interest.'

9.16 These factors give the court a very wide discretion in relation to its additional
powers and duties in making costs orders. In cases where there is a very wealthy paying
party, the judge may have come to a very clear view of how much the recipient needs,
and made his order accordingly. It may be manifest that the payor is comfortably able
to pay the costs of both parties without difficulty. However, to make the payee part with
a significant part of the lump sum which the judge has just awarded may throw out the
very calculations which the judge has made, thereby leaving the payee under provided.
How 'hard' are judges going to be in these circumstances? We shall have to wait and
see.

CHAPTER 10 –MISCELLANEOUS PROVISIONS

Applications for interim orders

10.01 Rule 2.69F provides that:
'(1)   A party may apply at any stage of the proceedings for an order for
        maintenance pending suit, interim periodical payments or an interim
        variation order.
(2)   An application for such an order must be made by notice of application
        and the date fixed for the hearing of the application must not be less than
        14 days after the date of the notice of application is issued.
(3)   The applicant shall forthwith serve the respondent with a copy of the
        notice of application'

10.02 Therefore, the soonest that an application for maintenance pending suit could
be heard within an ongoing application for ancillary relief would be 14 days after the
issue of Form A, if a court date was available so quickly, and if an application is made
by the applicant on the same day as the filing of form A.

10.03 If the application is made before Forms E have been filed and exchanged, it is
necessary to file with the application and serve on the other party a draft of the order
requested and a short sworn statement explaining the necessity for the order and giving
the necessary information [our italics] about his means, unless he has already filed
Form E[1]. No later than 7 days before the date of the hearing the respondent to this
application must similarly file and serve a short sworn statement of his means in the
absence of Form E.

1   Rule 2.69F (4).

10.04 It may be frustrating if there is no tactical advantage to be had by retaining Form
E, and it has already been prepared, to have to go to the expense of producing from it
an additional statement of means. However, Rule 2.61B is quite clear, and so this must
be done. It may, as we have already seen, be possible to combine the First Appointment

with a hearing of the interim application, and for a judge to make an interim order at that time[1].

1   Rule 2.61D(f)(i).

10.05 Applications for any other type of order may be made with or without notice[1], but if they are made with notice, then the provisions of paragraphs (1) – (5) relating to the filing of evidence apply[2].

1   Rule 2.69F(6).
2   Rule 2.69F(7).

10.06 Rules 18 to 23 of the Amended Rules are recited in full in Appendix A[1], and deal with the omission of various of the 1991 Rules, and the substitution of new terminology within those which remain.

1   See pp 68–69.

... AND FINALLY – THE PRE-APPLICATION PROTOCOL

10.07 In his Access to justice Report of July 1996, Lord Woolf recommended the development of pre-application protocols. By these instruments, he intended to regulate the use and conduct of any disclosure and negotiation which takes place before any proceedings are issued, in the hope of encouraging settlement without the need of the intervention of a court.

10.08 In April, 2000, the Lord Chancellor's Ancillary Relief Advisory Committee recommended that there be a Protocol which should be adopted before ancillary relief applications, which recommendation has been accepted by the Lord Chancellor.

10.09 The Protocol has not yet come into effect, but we have been given permission to reproduce it in its approved form, and do so at Appendix C[1].

1. See p 103 ff.

APPENDIX A

SI 1999 No 3491

Family Proceedings (Amendment No 2) Rules 1999

Made   15 December 1999
Laid before Parliament 14 January 2000
Coming into force   5 June 2000

We, the authority having the power under section 40(1) of the Matrimonial and Family Proceedings Act 1984 to make rules of court for the purposes of family proceedings in the High Court and county courts, in the exercise of the powers conferred by section 40 make the following rules—

Citation, commencement and transitional provisions

1

(1)   These rules may be cited as the Family Proceedings (Amendment No 2) Rules 1999 and shall come into force on 5th June 2000.

(2)   The Family Proceedings Rules 1991, as amended by these rules, shall apply to proceedings commenced by Form A or B on or after 5th June 2000.

(3)   Where proceedings have been commenced before 5th June 2000:

    (a)   the court may, if it considers it just to do so, direct that the Family Proceedings Rules 1991, as amended by these rules, shall apply to those proceedings; otherwise

    (b)   the Family Proceedings Rules 1991 shall apply to those proceedings as if these rules had not been made.

Amendment of the Family Proceedings Rules 1991

2

The Family Proceedings Rules 1991 shall be amended in accordance with the provisions of these rules.

3

In the Arrangement of Rules, for the numbers and words from "2.52 Right to be heard on ancillary questions" to "2.68 Application for order under section 37(2)(a) of Act of 1973", there shall be substituted the following;

"2.51A	Application of ancillary relief rules
2.51B	The overriding objective
2.52	Right to be heard on ancillary questions
2.53	Application by petitioner or respondent for ancillary relief
2.54	Application by parent, guardian etc for ancillary relief in respect of children
2.57	Children to be separately represented on certain applications
2.59	Evidence on application for property adjustment or avoidance of disposition order
2.60	Service of statement in answer
2.61	Information on application for consent order for financial relief
2.61A	Application for ancillary relief
2.61B	Procedure before the first appointment

4

(1)   In rule 1.2(4), after "Appendix 1" there shall be inserted "or 1A".

(2)   After rule 1.2(5) there shall be inserted:

"(5A)   In these rules a reference to a Part or rule, if prefixed by the letters "CPR", is
a reference to that Part or rule in the Civil Procedure Rules 1998.".

5

(1)   In rule 2.45(1) for "Form M12" there shall be substituted "Form B".

(2)   Rule 2.45(2) and (3) shall be omitted.

(3)   In rule 2.45(5):

(a)   the words "the proper officer shall fix an appointment for the hearing; and" shall
be omitted;

(b)   for "rules 2.62(3) to (7)" there shall be substituted "rules 2.51B to 2.70"; and

(c)   after "application for ancillary relief" there shall be inserted "and, unless the
context otherwise requires, those rules shall be read as if all references to Form
A were references to Form B".

6

Before rule 2.52, but after the heading "Ancillary relief," the following shall be inserted:

"Application of ancillary relief rules

2.51A

(1)   The procedures set out in rules 2.51B to 2.70 ("the ancillary relief rules") apply to any
ancillary relief application and to any application under section 10(2) of the Act of 1973.

(2)   In the ancillary relief rules, unless the context otherwise requires:

"applicant" means the party applying for ancillary relief;

"respondent" means the respondent to the application for ancillary relief;

"FDR appointment" means a Financial Dispute Resolution appointment in accordance with rule 2.61E.

The overriding objective

2.51B

(1)   The ancillary relief rules are a procedural code with the overriding objective of enabling the court to deal with cases justly.

(2)   Dealing with a case justly includes, so far as is practicable—

    (a)   ensuring that the parties are on an equal footing;

    (b)   saving expense;

    (c)   dealing with the case in ways which are proportionate—

        (i)   to the amount of money involved;

        (ii)   to the importance of the case;

        (iii)   to the complexity of the issues; and

        (iv)   to the financial position of each party;

    (d)   ensuring that it is dealt with expeditiously and fairly; and

    (e)   allotting to it an appropriate share of the court's resources, while taking into account the need to allot resources to other cases.

(3)   The court must seek to give effect to the overriding objective when it—

    (a)   exercises any power given to it by the ancillary relief rules; or

    (b)   interprets any rule.

(4)   The parties are required to help the court to further the overriding objective.

(5)   The court must further the overriding objective by actively managing cases.

(6)   Active case management includes—

    (a)   encouraging the parties to co-operate with each other in the conduct of the proceedings;

    (b)   encouraging the parties to settle their disputes through mediation, where appropriate;

    (c)   identifying the issues at an early date;

    (d)   regulating the extent of disclosure of documents and expert evidence so that they are proportionate to the issues in question;

    (e)   helping the parties to settle the whole or part of the case;

    (f)   fixing timetables or otherwise controlling the progress of the case;

    (g)   making use of technology; and

    (h)   giving directions to ensure that the trial of a case proceeds quickly and efficiently.".

7

In rule 2.53 and 2.54(1), for "Form M11", wherever it occurs, there shall be substituted "Form A".

8

Rules 2.55, 2.56 and 2.58 shall be omitted.

9

(1)   Rule 2.59(1) shall be omitted.

(2)   In rule 2.59(2) for "Form M11 or M13" there shall be substituted "Form A".

(3)   In rule 2.59(3) for the words from "A copy" to "supporting affidavit" there shall be substituted "Copies of Form A and of Form E completed by the applicant".

(4)   In rule 2.59(4):

    (a)   for "Form M11 or M13 as the case may be" there shall be substituted "Form A";

    (b)   for "affidavit" there shall be substituted "Form E".

(5)   In rule 2.59(5):

    (a)   for "an affidavit" in sub-paragraph (a) there shall be substituted "copies of Forms A and E";

    (b)   for "an affidavit" in sub-paragraph (b) there shall be substituted "a copy of Form E"; and

    (c)   for "file an affidavit" there shall be substituted "file a statement".

(6)   At the end of rule 2.59(5), there shall be inserted the following:

    "(6)   A statement filed under paragraph (5) shall be sworn to be true.".

10

For rule 2.60 there shall be substituted:

"Service of statement in answer

2.60

(1)   Where a form or other document filed with the court contains an allegation of adultery or of an improper association with a named person ("the named person"), the court may direct that the party who filed the relevant form or document serve a copy of all or part of that form or document on the named person, together with Form F.

(2)   If the court makes a direction under paragraph (1), the named person may file a statement in answer to the allegations.

(3)   A statement under paragraph (2) shall be sworn to be true.

(4)   Rule 2.37(3) shall apply to a person served under paragraph (1) as it applies to a co-respondent.".

11

After rule 2.61 there shall be inserted:

"Application for ancillary relief

2.61A

(1)   A notice of intention to proceed with an application for ancillary relief made in the petition or answer or an application for ancillary relief must be made by notice in Form A.

(2)   The notice must be filed:

    (a)   if the case is pending in a divorce county court, in that court; or

    (b)   if the case is pending in the High Court, in the registry in which it is proceeding.

(3)   Where the applicant requests an order for ancillary relief that includes provision to be made by virtue of section 25B or 25C of the Act of 1973 the terms of the order requested must be specified in the notice in Form A.

(4)   Upon the filing of Form A the court must:

    (a)   fix a first appointment not less than 12 weeks and not more than 16 weeks after the date of the filing of the notice and give notice of that date;

    (b)   serve a copy on the respondent within 4 days of the date of the filing of the notice.

(5)   The date fixed under paragraph (4) for the first appointment, or for any subsequent appointment, must not be cancelled except with the court's permission and, if cancelled, the court must immediately fix a new date.

Procedure before the first appointment

2.61B

(1)   Both parties must, at the same time, exchange with each other, and each file with the court, a statement in Form E, which—

    (a)   is signed by the party who made the statement;

    (b)   is sworn to be true, and

    (c)   contains the information and has attached to it the documents required by that Form.

(2)   Form E must be exchanged and filed not less than 35 days before the date of the first appointment.

(3)   Form E must have attached to it:

    (a)   any documents required by Form E; and

    (b)   any other documents necessary to explain or clarify any of the information contained in Form E.

(4)   Form E must have no documents attached to it other than the documents referred to in paragraph (3).

(5)   Where a party was unavoidably prevented from sending any document required by Form E, that party must at the earliest opportunity:

    (a)   serve copies of that document on the other party; and

    (b)   file a copy of that document with the court, together with a statement explaining the failure to send it with Form E.

(6)   No disclosure or inspection of documents may be requested or given between the filing of the application for ancillary relief and the first appointment, except—

    (a)   copies sent with Form E, or in accordance with paragraph (5); or

    (b)   in accordance with paragraph (7).

(7)   At least 14 days before the hearing of the first appointment, each party must file with the court and serve on the other party—

    (a)   a concise statement of the issues between the parties;

    (b)   a chronology;

    (c)   a questionnaire setting out by reference to the concise statement of issues any further information and documents requested from the other party or a statement that no information and documents are required;

    (d)   a notice in Form G stating whether that party will be in a position at the first appointment to proceed on that occasion to a FDR appointment.

(8)   Where an order for ancillary relief is requested that includes provision to be made under section 25B or 25C of the Act of 1973, the applicant must file with the court and serve on the respondent at least 14 days before the hearing of the first appointment, confirmation that rule 2.70(4) has been complied with.

(9)   At least 14 days before the hearing of the first appointment, the applicant must file with the court and serve on the respondent, confirmation of the names of all persons served in accordance with rule 2.59(3) and (4), and that there are no other persons who must be served in accordance with those paragraphs.

Expert evidence

2.61C

CPR rules 35.1 to 35.14 relating to expert evidence (with appropriate modifications), except CPR rules 35.5(2) and 35.8(4)(b) apply to all ancillary relief proceedings.

The first appointment

2.61D

(1)   The first appointment must be conducted with the objective of defining the issues and saving costs.

(2)   At the first appointment the district judge—

    (a)   must determine—

        (i)   the extent to which any questions seeking information under rule 2.61B must be answered; and

        (ii)   what documents requested under rule 2.61B must be produced,

    and give directions for the production of such further documents as may be necessary;

    (b)   must give directions about—

        (i)   the valuation of assets (including, where appropriate, the joint instruction of joint experts);

        (ii)   obtaining and exchanging expert evidence, if required; and

        (iii)   evidence to be adduced by each party and, where appropriate, about further chronologies or schedules to be filed by each party;

    (c)   must, unless he decides that a referral is not appropriate in the circumstances, direct that the case be referred to a FDR appointment;

    (d)   must, where he decides that a referral to a FDR appointment is not appropriate, direct one of the following:

        (i)   that a further directions appointment be fixed;

        (ii)   that an appointment be fixed for the making of an interim order;

        (iii)   that the case be fixed for final hearing and, where that direction is given, the district judge must determine the judicial level at which the case should be heard; or

        (iv)   that the case be adjourned for out-of-court mediation or private negotiation or, in exceptional circumstances, generally;

    (e)   must consider whether, having regard to all the circumstances (including the extent to which each party has complied with this Part, and in particular the requirement to send documents with Form E), to make an order about the costs of the hearing; and

(f)   may—

    (i)   make an interim order where an application for it has been made in accordance with rule 2.69F returnable at the first appointment;

    (ii)   having regard to the contents of Form G filed by the parties, treat the appointment (or part of it) as a FDR appointment to which rule 2.61E applies;

    (iii)   in a case where an order for ancillary relief is requested that includes provision to be made under section 25B or 25C of the Act of 1973, require any party to request a valuation under regulation 4 of the Divorce etc (Pensions) Regulations 1996 from the trustees or managers of any pension scheme under which the party has, or is likely to have, any benefits.

(3)   After the first appointment, a party is not entitled to production of any further documents except in accordance with directions given under paragraph (2)(a) above or with the permission of the court.

(4)   At any stage:

    (a)   a party may apply for further directions or a FDR appointment;

    (b)   the court may give further directions or direct that the parties attend a FDR appointment.

(5)   Both parties must personally attend the first appointment unless the court orders otherwise.

The FDR appointment

2.61E

(1)   The FDR appointment must be treated as a meeting held for the purposes of discussion and negotiation and paragraphs (2) to (9) apply.

(2)   The district judge or judge hearing the FDR appointment must have no further involvement with the application, other than to conduct any further FDR appointment or to make a consent order or a further directions order.

(3)   Not later than 7 days before the FDR appointment, the applicant must file with the court details of all offers and proposals, and responses to them.

(4)   Paragraph (3) includes any offers, proposals or responses made wholly or partly without prejudice, but paragraph (3) does not make any material admissible as evidence if, but for that paragraph, it would not be admissible.

(5)   At the conclusion of the FDR appointment, any documents filed under paragraph (3), and any filed documents referring to them, must, at the request of the party who filed them, be returned to him and not retained on the court file.

(6)   Parties attending the FDR appointment must use their best endeavours to reach agreement on the matters in issue between them.

(7)   The FDR appointment may be adjourned from time to time.

(8)   At the conclusion of the FDR appointment, the court may make an appropriate consent order, but otherwise must give directions for the future course of the proceedings, including, where appropriate, the filing of evidence and fixing a final hearing date.

(9)   Both parties must personally attend the FDR appointment unless the court orders otherwise.

Costs

2.61F

(1)   At every court hearing or appointment each party must produce to the court an estimate in Form H of the costs incurred by him up to the date of that hearing or appointment.

(2)   The parties' obligation under paragraph (1) is without prejudice to their obligations under paragraphs 4.1 to 4.11 of the Practice Direction relating to CPR Part 44.".

12

(1)   Rule 2.62(1), (3), (5) and (6) shall be omitted.

(2)   In rule 2.62(4):

    (a)   for "discovery and production" there shall be substituted "disclosure and inspection"; and

    (b)   for "affidavits" there shall be substituted "statements".

(3)   After rule 2.62(4), there shall be inserted:

"(4A)   A statement filed under paragraph (4) shall be sworn to be true.".

(4)   In rule 2.62(7):

    (a)   for "(a "production appointment")" there shall be substituted "(an "inspection appointment")"; and

    (b)   for the second occurrence of "production" there shall be substituted "inspection".

(5)   In rule 2.62(8), for "a production" there shall be substituted "an inspection".

(6)   In rule 2.62(9), for "a production" there shall be substituted "an inspection".

13

Rule 2.63 shall be omitted.

14

In rule 2.64(2) after "final determination of the application," there shall be substituted "and subject to rule 2.69F,".

15

In rule 2.66(4) for "as a district judge has under rule 2.62(5)" there shall be substituted "to make directions as a district judge has under these rules".

16

In rule 2.67(2) for "Form M15", wherever it occurs, there shall be substituted "Form I".

17

(1)   For rule 2.69 there shall be substituted:

"Offers to settle

2.69

(1)   Either party to the application may at any time make a written offer to the other party which is expressed to be "without prejudice except as to costs" and which relates to any issue in the proceedings relating to the application.

(2)   Where an offer is made under paragraph (1), the fact that such an offer has been made shall not be communicated to the court, except in accordance with rule 2.61E(3), until the question of costs falls to be decided.

Interpretation of rules 2.69B to 2.69D

2.69A

In rules 2.69B to 2.69D, "base rate" has the same meaning as in the Civil Procedure Rules 1998.

Judgment or order more advantageous than an offer made by the other party

2.69B

(1)　　This rule applies where the judgment or order in favour of the applicant or respondent is more advantageous to him than an offer made under rule 2.69(1) by the other party.

(2)　　The court must, unless it considers it unjust to do so, order that other party to pay any costs incurred after the date beginning 28 days after the offer was made.

Judgment or order more advantageous than offers made by both parties

2.69C

(1)　　This rule applies where

　　　　(a)　　both the applicant and the respondent have made offers under rule 2.69(1); and

　　　　(b)　　the judgment or order in favour of the applicant or the respondent, as the case may be, is more advantageous to him than both of the offers referred to in paragraph (a).

(2)　　The court may, where it considers it just, order interest in accordance with paragraph (3) on the whole or part of any sum of money (excluding interest and periodical payments) to be awarded to the applicant or respondent, as the case may be.

(3)　　Interest under paragraph (2) may be at a rate not exceeding 10 per cent above base rate for some or all of the period beginning 28 days after the offer was made.

(4)　　The court may also order that the applicant or respondent, as the case may be, is entitled to:

　　　　(a)　　his costs on the indemnity basis beginning 28 days after the offer was made; and

　　　　(b)　　interest on those costs at a rate not exceeding 10 per cent above base rate.

(5)　　The court's powers under this rule are in addition to its powers under rule 2.69B.

Factors for court's consideration under rules 2.69B and 2.69C

2.69D

(1)　　In considering whether it would be unjust, or whether it would be just, to make the orders referred to in rules 2.69B and 2.69C, the court must take into account all the circumstances of the case, including—

　　　　(a)　　the terms of any offers made under rule 2.69(1);

　　　　(b)　　the stage in the proceedings when any offer was made;

　　　　(c)　　the information available to the parties at the time when the offer was made;

　　　　(d)　　the conduct of the parties with regard to the giving or refusing to give information for the purposes of enabling the offer to be made or evaluated; and

　　　　(e)　　the respective means of the parties.

(2)　　The power of the court to award interest under rule 2.69C(2) and (4)(b) is in addition to any other power it may have to award interest.

Open proposals

2.69E

(1)   Not less than 14 days before the date fixed for the final hearing of an application for ancillary relief, the applicant must (unless the court directs otherwise) file with the court and serve on the respondent an open statement which sets out concise details, including the amounts involved, of the orders which he proposes to ask the court to make.

(2)   Not more than 7 days after service of a statement under paragraph (1), the respondent must file with the court and serve on the applicant an open statement which sets out concise details, including the amounts involved, of the orders which he proposes to ask the court to make.

Application for interim orders

2.69F

(1)   A party may apply at any stage of the proceedings for an order for maintenance pending suit, interim periodical payments or an interim variation order.

(2)   An application for such an order must be made by notice of application and the date fixed for the hearing of the application must be not less than 14 days after the date the notice of application is issued.

(3)   The applicant shall forthwith serve the respondent with a copy of the notice of application.

(4)   Where an application is made before a party has filed Form E, that party must file with the application and serve on the other party, a draft of the order requested and a short sworn statement explaining why the order is necessary and giving the necessary information about his means.

(5)   Not less than 7 days before the date fixed for the hearing, the respondent must file with the court and serve on the other party, a short sworn statement about his means, unless he has already filed Form E.

(6)   A party may apply for any other form of interim order at any stage of the proceedings with or without notice.

(7)   Where an application referred to in paragraph (6) is made with notice, the provisions of paragraphs (1) to (5) apply to it.

(8)   Where an application referred to in paragraph (6) is made without notice, the provisions of paragraph (1) apply to it.".

18

(1)   Rule 2.70(1) shall be omitted.

(2)   In rule 2.70(2) for "discovery" there shall be substituted "disclosure".

(3)   In rule 2.70(3):

    (a)   for sub-paragraph (a) there shall be substituted:

        "(a)   Form A in accordance with rule 2.61A; or";

    (b)   sub-paragraph (b) shall be omitted.

(4)   In rule 2.70(4) for "Form M11 or M13 as the case may be" there shall be substituted "Form A".

19

Rules 2.71 to 2.77 shall be omitted.

20

In Part III references to any of rules 2.52 to 2.70 shall be read as references to those rules as they were before these rules came into force.

21

In rule 3.1(7) for "intervention by" there shall be substituted "filing of a statement in answer by".

22

Forms M11 to M15 shall be omitted from Appendix 1.

23

The following shall be substituted for Appendix 1A:

"APPENDIX 1A

Notice of [intention to proceed with] an Application for Ancillary Relief

<table>
<tr><td colspan="2">In the

*[County Court]
*[Principal Registry of the Family Division]</td></tr>
<tr><td>Case No.
Always quote this</td><td></td></tr>
<tr><td>Applicant's Solicitor's reference</td><td></td></tr>
<tr><td>Respondent's Solicitor's reference</td><td></td></tr>
</table>

*(*delete as appropriate)*

Postcode

(Name and Address of Respondent(s) / Respondent(s) Solicitors)

The marriage of   **and**

Take Notice that

the Applicant intends **to apply** to the Court or

to proceed with the application in the [petition][answer] for:

☐ an order for maintenance pending suit   ☐ a periodical payments order
☐ a secured provision order   ☐ a lump sum order
☐ a property adjustment order

If an application is made for any periodical payments or secured periodical payments for children:

- and there is a written agreement made before 5 April 1993 about maintenance for the benefit of children, **tick this box**   ☐

- and there is a written agreement made on or after 5 April 1993 about maintenance for the benefit of children, **tick this box**   ☐

- but there is no agreement, tick any of the boxes below to show if you are applying for payment:

☐ for a stepchild or stepchildren
☐ in addition to child support maintenance already paid under a Child Support Agency assessment
☐ to meet expenses arising from a child's disability
☐ to meet expenses incurred by a child in being educated or training for work
☐ when either the child **or** the person with care of the child **or** the absent parent of the child is not habitually resident in the United Kingdom
☐ Other (please state)

Signed: Dated:

[Applicant/Solicitor for the Applicant]

The court office at

is open between 10 am and 4 pm (4.30pm at the Principal Registry of the Family Division) Monday to Friday. When corresponding with the court, please address forms or letters to the Court Manager and quote the case number. If you do not do so, your correspondence may be returned.

Form A Notice of [Intention to proceed with] an Application for Ancillary Relief

Notice of an application under Rule 2.45

In the	
[County Court] *[Principal Registry of the Family Division]*	
Case No. *Always quote this*	
Petitioner's Solicitor's reference	
Respondent's Solicitor's reference	

*(*delete as apprpriate)*

The marriage of   and

Take Notice that

The Respondent intends to apply to the Court under section 10(2) of the Matrimonial Causes Act 1973 for the Court to consider the financial position of the Respondent after the divorce.

Signed: Dated:

[Respondent/Solicitor for the Respondent]

The court office at

is open between 10 am and 4 pm (4.30pm at the Principal Registry of the Family Division) Monday to Friday. When corresponding with the court, please address forms or letters to the Court Manager and quote the case number. If you do not do so, your correspondence may be returned.

Form B Notice of an Application under Rule 2.45

Notice of a First Appointment

In the	
*[County Court] *[Principal Registry of the Family Division]	
Case No. *Always quote this*	
Applicant's Solicitor's reference	
Respondent's Solicitor's reference	

*(*delete as appropriate)*

The marriage of   **and**

Take Notice that

By [**]** you must file with the Court a statement which gives full details of your property and income. You must sign and swear the statement. At the same time each party must exchange a copy of the statement with the [legal representative of the] other party. You must use the standard form of statement (Form E) which you may obtain from the Court office.

By [**]** you must file with the Court and the [legal representative of the] other party:

- a concise statement of the apparent issues between yourself and the other party;
- a chronology;
- a questionnaire setting out the further information and documents you require from the other party, or a statement that no information or documents are required;
- a Notice in Form G.

The First Appointment will be heard by

(the District Judge in chambers) at

on   20

at   [a.m.][p.m.]

The probable length of the hearing is

> **You and your legal representative, if you have one, must attend the appointment. At the appointment you must provide the Court with a written estimate (in Form H) of any legal costs which you have incurred. Non-compliance may render you liable to costs penalties.**

Dated:

The court office at

is open between 10 am and 4 pm (4.30pm at the Principal Registry of the Family Division) Monday to Friday. When corresponding with the court, please address forms or letters to the Court Manager and quote the case number. If you do not do so, your correspondence may be returned.

Form C Notice of a First Appointment

Notice of a Financial Dispute Resolution Appointment

In the	
	*[County Court]
	*[Principal Registry of the Family Division]
Case No. *Always quote this*	
Applicant's Solicitor's reference	
Respondent's Solicitor's reference	

*(*delete as appropriate)*

The marriage of   **and**

Take Notice that

By [**]** the Applicant must provide the Court with details of all offers, proposals and responses concerning the Application.

An appointment for a Financial Dispute Resolution will take place at

on   20

at   [a.m.][p.m.]

The probable length of the hearing is

At the appointment

* You, and your legal representative, if you have one, must attend this appointment.
* The hearing will define, as far as possible, the issues in this matter and explore the possibility of settlement. If the matter proceeds to a full hearing, the date of the full hearing will be fixed.
* You must provide the Court with a written estimate (in Form H) of any legal costs.

Dated:

The court office at

is open between 10 am and 4 pm (4.30pm at the Principal Registry of the Family Division) Monday to Friday. When corresponding with the court, please address forms or letters to the Court Manager and quote the case number. If you do not do so, your correspondence may be returned.

Form D Notice of a Financial Dispute Resolution Appointment

FINANCIAL STATEMENT

*Applicant/*Respondent

In the	
	*[County Court]
*[Principal Registry of the Family Division]	
Case No *Always quote this*	

(delete as appropriate)

Between | Applicant | and | Respondent
| | |
| Solicitor's Ref: | | Solicitor's Ref: |

Please fill in this form fully and accurately. Where any box is not applicable write "N/A". You have a duty to the court to give a full, frank and clear disclosure of all your financial and other relevant circumstances.

A failure to give full and accurate disclosure may result in any order the court makes being set aside.

If you are found to have been deliberately untruthful, criminal proceedings for perjury may be taken against you.

You must attach documents to the form where they are specifically sought and you may attach other documents where it is necessary to explain or clarify any of the information that you give.

Essential documents, which **must** accompany this Statement, are detailed at questions 2.1, 2.2, 2.3, 2.5, 2.14, 2.18 and 2.20.

If there is not enough room on the form for any particular piece of information, you may continue on an attached sheet of paper.

This statement must be sworn before an Officer of the Court
or a Commissioner for Oaths
before it is filed with the Court
or sent to the other party
(see page 20).

Part 1 General Information

1.1 Full Name

1.2 Date of Birth

Date	Month	Year

1.3 Date of Marriage

Date	Month	Year

1.4 Occupation

1.5 Date of the separation

Date	Month	Year

Tick here ☐ if not applicable

1.6 Date of the:

Petition			Decree Nisi/Decree of Judicial Separation			Decree Absolute		
Date	Month	Year	Date	Month	Year	Date	Month	Year

1.7 If you have remarried, or will remarry, state the date

Date	Month	Year

1.8 Do you live with another person? ☐ Yes ☐ No

1.9 Do you intend to live with someone within the next six months? ☐ Yes ☐ No

1.10 Details of any children of the family

Full names	Date of Birth			With whom does the child live?
	Date	Month	Year	

1.11 Give details of the state of health of yourself and the children

Yourself	Children

1.12 Give details of the present and proposed future educational arrangements for the children.

Present arrangements	Future arrangements

1.13 Give details of any Child Support Maintenance Assessments or Child Maintenance Orders made between the parties. If no assessment or agreement has been made, give an estimate of the liability of the non-residential parent under the Child Support Act 1991, in respect of the children of the family.

1.14 If this application is to vary an order, give details of the order that is to be varied and attach a copy of the order. Give the reasons for asking for the order to be varied.

1.15 Give details of any other court cases between you and your husband/wife, whether in relation to money, property, children or anything else.

Case No	Court

1.16 Specify your present residence and the occupants of it and on what terms you occupy it (e.g. tenant, owner-occupier).

Address	Occupants	Terms of occupation

Part 2 Financial Details   *Capital: Realisable Assets*

*If you have obtained a valuation within the last six months attach a copy. If not, give your own estimate of the property value. A copy of your most recent mortgage statement is also required.

2.1 Give details of your interest in the matrimonial home.

Property name and address	Land Registry Title No.	Nature and extent of your interest	*Property value

Mortgagee's Name and address	Type of mortgage	Balance outstanding on any mortgage	Total current value of your beneficial interest
1st			
2nd			
Other:			

NET value of your interest in the matrimonial home (A)	£

2.2 Give details of all other properties, land, and buildings in which you have an interest

Property name(s) and address(es)	Land Registry Title No.	Nature and extent of your interest	*Property value
1.			
2.			
3.			

Mortgagee's Name(s) and address(es)	Type of mortgage	Balance outstanding on any mortgage	Total current value of your interest
1.			
2.			
3.			

TOTAL value of the above (not including the matrimonial home)	(B1) £

2.3 Give details of all bank, building society, and National Savings accounts, in credit, which you hold or have an interest in. Include all PEPs, TESSAs and ISAs. For joint accounts, give your interest and the name of the account holder. If the account is overdrawn, include in Liabilities section at 2.12

You must attach your bank statements covering the last 12 months for each account listed

Name of bank or building society including Branch name	Type of account (e.g. current)	Account number	Name of other account holder *(if applicable)*	Balance at the date of this Statement	Total current value of your interest
1.					
2.					
3.					
4.					
5.					
			TOTAL value of your interest in ALL accounts		(B2) £

2.4 Give details of all stocks, gilts and other quoted securities which you hold or have an interest in. Do not include dividend income as this will be dealt with separately later on

Name	Type	Size	Current value	Total current value of your interest
			TOTAL value of your interest in ALL holdings	(B3) £

2.5 Give details of all life insurance policies which you hold or in which you have an interest, including those that do not have a surrender value, for each policy.

Policy details including name of company, policy type and number	If policy is charged, state in whose favour and amount of charge	Maturity date			Surrender Value	Total current value of your interest
		Date	Month	Year		
You must attach any surrender value quotations		TOTAL value of your interest in ALL policies				(B4) £

2.6 Give details of all issues of National Savings Certificates which you hold or have an interest in.

Name of issue	Nominal amount	Current value	Total current value of your interest

TOTAL value of ALL your certificates

(B5)
£

2.7 Give details of all of National Savings Bonds (including Premium bonds) and other bonds which you hold or have an interest in.

Type of Bond	Bond holder's number	Current value	Total current value of your interest

TOTAL value of ALL your bonds

(B6)
£

2.8 Give details of all monies which are OWED TO YOU. Include sums owed in director's or partnership accounts

Brief description of debt	Balance outstanding	Total current value of your interest

TOTAL value of your interest in ALL debts owed to you

(B7)
£

2.9 Give details of all of cash savings held in excess of £300. You must state where it is held and the currency it is held in.

Where held	Amount	Currency	Total current value of your interest

	(B8)
TOTAL value of ALL your cash	£

2.10 Give details of personal belongings individually worth more than £500.
Include cars (gross value), collections, pictures, jewellery, furniture, and household belongings (this list is not exhaustive).

Item	Sale value	Total estimated current value of your interest

	(B9)
TOTAL value of your interest in ALL personal belongings	£

2.11 Give details of any other realisable assets not yet mentioned, for example, unit trusts, investment trusts, commodities, business expansion schemes and futures (this list is not exhaustive). This is where you must mention any other realisable assets.

Type	Current value	Total current value of your interest

	(B10)
TOTAL value of your interest in ALL other realisable assets	£

Now add together all the figures in the previous total boxes (B1 to B10) to give the TOTAL current value of ALL your interest in realisable assets.

(B) £

7

Part 2 Financial Details   *Capital: Liabilities*

2.12 Give details of any liabilities you have. Exclude mortgages on property dealt with above.
Include money owed on credit cards and store cards, bank loans, hire purchase agreements and any
overdrawn bank or building society accounts.

Liability (i.e. total amount owed, current monthly payments and term of loan/debt)	Current amount	Total current value of your share of the liability
TOTAL value of ALL your liabilities		(C1) £

Part 2 Financial Details   *Capital: Capital Gains Tax*

2.13 If any Capital Gains Tax would be payable on the disposal now of any of your realisable assets,
give your estimate of the tax.

Asset	Capital Gains Tax	Total current value of your liability
TOTAL value of ALL your Capital Gains Tax liabilities		(C2) £

Now add together C1 + C2 to give:- TOTAL net value of your liabilities	**(C)**	£

Now take the liabilities total from the realisable assets total (A+B-C), to give:- TOTAL net value of your personal assets	**(D)**	£

8

Part 2 Financial Details   *Capital: Business Assets*

2.14 Give details of all your business interests.   *You must attach a copy of the last 2 years accounts and any other document on which you base your valuation.*

Name and nature of your business	Your ESTIMATE of the current value of your interest	Your ESTIMATE of any possible Capital Gains Tax payable on disposal	Basis of valuation *(No formal valuation is required at this time)*	What is the extent of your interest?	Total net current value of your interest

TOTAL current value of your interest in business assets   (E)   £

2.15 List any directorships you hold or held in the last 12 months

Part 2 Financial Details

Capital: Pensions *(including SERPS but excluding Basic State Pensions)*

2.16 Give details of your pension interests.

If you have been provided with a valuation of your pension rights by the trustees or managers of the pension scheme you must attach it. Where the information is not available, give the estimated date when it will be available and attach the letter to the pension company or administrators from whom the information was sought. If you have more than one pension plan or scheme, you must provide the information in respect of each one, continuing, if necessary, on a separate piece of paper. If you have made Additional Voluntary Contributions or any Free Standing Additional Voluntary Contributions to any plan or scheme, you must give the information separately if the benefits referable to such contributions are separately recorded or paid. If you have more than one pension scheme you should reproduce the information for each scheme. Please include any SERPS.

Information about the Scheme(s)

Name and address of scheme, plan or policy	
Number of scheme, plan or policy	
Type of scheme, plan or policy *(e.g. final salary, money purchase or other)*	

CETV - Cash Equivalent Transfer Value

CETV Value	
The lump sum payable on death in service before retirement	
The lump sum payable on death in deferment before retirement	
The lump sum payable on death after retirement	

Retirement Benefits

Earliest date when benefit can be paid	
The estimated lump sum and monthly pension payable on retirement, assuming you take the maximum lump sum	
The estimated monthly pension without taking any lump sum	

Spouse's Benefit

On death in service	
On death in deferment	
On death in retirement	

Dependant's Benefit

On death in service	
On death in deferment	
On death in retirement	

TOTAL value of your pension assets (F) £

10

Part 2 Financial Details   *Capital: Other Assets*

2.17 Give details of any other assets not listed above.
Include the following: (this list is not exhaustive)

* **Unrealisable assets.**
* **Share option scheme**, stating the estimated net sale proceeds of the shares if the options were capable of exercise now, and whether Capital Gains Tax or Income Tax would be payable.
* **Trust interests** (including interests under a discretionary trust), stating your estimate of the value of the interest and when it is likely to become realisable. If you say it will never be realisable, or has no value, give your reasons.
* Specify also any asset that is likely to be received in the forseeable future, any assets held on your behalf by a third party and any assets not mentioned elsewhere in this form held outside England and Wales.

Type of Asset	Value	Total net value of your interest

Total value of your other assets **(G)**	£
Total value of your net assets (excluding pensions) **(D+E+G) (H)**	£
Total value of your net assets (including pension) **(H+F) (I)**	£

Part 2 Financial Details   *Income*   *You must attach your last three payslips and your P60 for the most recently completed financial year*

2.18 Earned Income: Give details of your gross and net income in the last financial year, and in the current financial year.

Nature of income (e.g. salary, bonus)	Last financial year		Current financial year *(estimated for the whole year)*	
	Gross	Net	Gross	Net

2.19 Additional Income: benefits etc. Give details and the value of all benefits in kind, perks, or other remuneration not disclosed elsewhere, received in the last financial year and current financial year.

Nature of income	Last financial year	Current financial year *(estimated for the whole year)*

12

Income continued

2.20 Self-employed or partnership income: Give details of annual net profit or loss for the last two accounting years, your share of this figure and tax payable to date of the last accounts and the estimate of income since that date. State the date on which your accounting year begins. Year 2 should be the most recent year, Year 1 the previous year. Please state the "from" and "to" dates for the years concerned.

Nature of income and date your accounting year begins	Details of the last two accounting periods					
	Net profit/loss		Your share of profit/loss		Tax payable by you	
	Year 1	Year 2	Year 1	Year 2	Year 1	Year 2

	Net Income	Estimate	
Net income SINCE date of last accounts and estimate for the whole year			*You must attach the accounts for the last two completed accounting years*

2.21 Investment income (e.g. dividends, interest) Give details of net income received in the last financial year, and in the current financial year and state whether it was paid gross or net of income tax. You are not required to calculate any tax payable that may arise.

Nature of income and the asset from which it derived	Paid gross or net (*delete that which is not applicable*)	Last financial year	Current financial year
	Gross / Net		

2.22 State benefits (including state pension) Give details of all state benefits received in the last 52 weeks

Nature of income	Total Income received in the last 52 weeks

2.23 Any other income Give details of any other income received in the last 52 weeks

Nature of income	Total Income for the last 52 weeks

Part 2 Financial Details *Summaries*

2.24 Summary of your income

Your estimate of your current annual net income from all sources (2.18 - 2.23)	Your estimate of your net income from all sources for the next 52 weeks
£	£ **(J)**

2.25 Summary of financial information

	Reference of the section on this statement	Value
Net value of your interest in the matrimonial home	A	
Total current value of all your your interest in the other realisable assets	B	
Total net value of your liabilities	C	
Total net value of your personal assets	D	
Total current value of your interest in business assets	E	
Total current value of your pension or transfer values	F	
Total value of your other assets	G	
Total value of your net assets *(excluding pension)*	H	
Total value of your net assets *(including pension)*	I	
Your estimated net income for the next 52 weeks	J	

14

Part 3 Requirements   *Income Needs*

3.1   Give the reasonable future income needs of yourself (e.g. housing, car etc) and of any children living with you, or provided for by you. This may be expressed as annual, monthly or weekly figures (state which), but you should not use a combination of any of these periods.

Item	Income needs of yourself	Amount
	sub-total	

Item	Income needs of child(ren) living with you, or provided for by you.	Amount
	sub-total	
	Total income needs	£

Part 3 Requirements   *Capital Needs*

3.2 Give the reasonable future capital needs of yourself and of any children living with you, or provided for by you.

Item	*Capital needs of yourself*	Cost
	sub-total	

Item	*Capital needs of child(ren) living with you, or provided for by you.*	Cost
	sub-total	
	Total capital needs	£

Part 4 Other Information

4.1 State whether there has been any significant change in your net assets during the last 12 months, including any assets held outside England and Wales (e.g. closure of any bank or building society accounts).

4.2 Give brief details of the standard of living enjoyed by you and your spouse during the marriage.

4.3 Are there any particular contributions to the family property and assets or outgoings, or to family life, that have been made by you, your partner or anyone else that you think should be taken into account? If so, give a brief description of the contribution, the amount, when it was made, and by whom.

4.4 Bad behaviour or conduct by the other party will only be taken into account in very exceptional circumstances when deciding how the assets should be divided after divorce. If you feel it should be taken into account in your case identify the nature of the behaviour or conduct.

Part 4 Other Information   *continued*

4.5   Give details of any other circumstances which you consider could significantly affect the extent of the financial provision to be made by or for you or for any child of the family e.g. earning capacity, disability, inheritance prospects or redundancy, remarriage and cohabitation plans, any contingent liabilities. (This list is not exhaustive).

4.6   If you have remarried (or intend to) or are living with another person (or intend to), give brief details, so far as they are known to you, of his or her income and assets.

Annual Income		Assets	
Nature of income	Value (state whether gross or net, if known)	Item	Value (if known)
Total:		**Total:**	

18

Part 5 Order Sought

5.1   If you are able to at this stage, specify what kind of orders you are asking the court to make, and state whether at this stage you see the case being appropriate for a "clean break". (A "clean break" means a settlement or order which provides, amongst other things, that neither you nor your spouse will have any further claim against the income or capital of the other party. A clean break does not terminate the responsibility of a parent to a child).

5.2   **If you are seeking a transfer or settlement of any property or other asset, you must identify the asset in question.

5.3   **If you are seeking a variation of a pre-nuptial or post-nuptial settlement, you must identify the settlement, by whom it was made, its trustees and beneficiaries, and state why you allege it is a nuptial settlement.

**   **Important Note:** Where 5.2, 5.3 (above) or 5.4 (overleaf) apply, you should seek legal advice before completing the sections.

Part 5 Order Sought   *continued*

5.4   **If you are seeking an avoidance of disposition order, you must identify the property to which the disposition relates and the person or body in whose favour the disposition is alleged to have been made.**

Sworn confirmation of the information

I

(the above-named Applicant/Respondent)

of

make oath and confirm that the information given above is a full, frank, clear and accurate disclosure of my financial and other relevant circumstances.

Signed

Dated

Sworn by the above named [Applicant] [Respondent] at

on

before me

A [solicitor] [Commissioner for Oaths] [Officer of a Court, appointed by the Judge to take Affidavits]

Address all communications to the Court Manager of the Court and quote the case number from page 1. If you do not quote this number, your correspondence may be returned.

The court office at

is open from 10 a.m. to 4p.m. (4.30pm at the Principal Registry of the Family Division) on Monday to Friday only.

Notice of Allegation in Proceedings for Ancillary Relief

In the	
*[County Court] *[Principal Registry of the Family Division]	
Case No. *Always quote this*	
Applicant's Solicitor's reference	
Respondent's Solicitor's reference	

(*delete as appropriate)

The marriage of   and

Take Notice that

The following statement has been filed in proceedings for ancillary relief:

Signed: Dated:

[Applicant / Respondent/Solicitor for the Applicant / Respondent]

If you wish to be heard on any matter affecting you in these proceedings you may intervene by applying to the Court for directions regarding:

- the filing and service of pleadings
- the conduct of further proceedings

You must apply for directions **within seven days** after you receive this Notice. The period of seven days includes the day you receive it.

The court office at

is open between 10 am and 4 pm (4.30pm at the Principal Registry of the Family Division) Monday to Friday. When corresponding with the court, please address forms or letters to the Court Manager and quote the case number. If you do not do so, your correspondence may be returned.

Form F Notice of allegation in proceedings for ancillary relief

Notice of response to First Appointment

In the	
*[County Court] *[Principal Registry of the Family Division]	
Case No. *Always quote this*	
Applicant's Solicitor's reference	
Respondent's Solicitor's reference	

(*delete as appropriate)

The marriage of   and

Take Notice that

At the First Appointment which will be heard on   20

at   [am][pm]

the [Applicant] [Respondent] [will][will not] be in a position to proceed on that occasion with a Financial Dispute Resolution appointment for the following reasons:-

Dated:

The court office at

is open between 10 am and 4 pm (4.30pm at the Principal Registry of the Family Division) Monday to Friday. When corresponding with the court, please address forms or letters to the Court Manager and quote the case number. If you do not do so, your correspondence may be returned.

Form G Notice of response to First Appointment

Ancillary Relief
Costs Estimate of
*[Applicant]
*[Respondent]

In the	
*[County Court] *[Principal Registry of the Family Division]	
Case No. *Always quote this*	
Applicant's Solicitor's reference	
Respondent's Solicitor's reference	

*(*delete as appropriate)*

The marriage of   **and**

PART 1

	Legal Aid Rates £	Indemnity Rate £
1. Ancillary relief solicitor's costs *(including VAT)* including costs of the current hearing, and any previous solicitor's costs.		
2. Disbursements *(include VAT, if appropriate, and any incurred by previous solicitors)*		
3. All Counsel's fees *(including VAT)*		
TOTAL		

PART 2

4. Add any private cases costs previously incurred *(Legal Aid cases only)*		
5. **GRAND TOTAL**		

PART 3

6. State what has been paid towards the total at 5 above		
7. Amount of any contributions paid by the assisted person towards their legal aid certificate		

NB. If you are Legally Aided and might be seeking an order for costs against the other party complete both rates.

Dated

The court office at

is open between 10 am and 4 pm (4.30pm at the Principal Registry of the Family Division) Monday to Friday. When corresponding with the court, please address forms or letters to the Court Manager and quote the case number. If you do not do so, your correspondence may be returned.

Form H Costs Estimate

Notice of Request for Periodical Payments Order at same rate as Order for Maintenance Pending Suit

In the	
*[County Court] *[Principal Registry of the Family Division]**	
Case No. Always quote this	
Applicant's Solicitor's reference	
Respondent's Solicitor's reference	

(*delete as appropriate)

Tho marriage of   and

Take Notice that

On   1999 [20   ] the Applicant obtained an Order for you to pay maintenance pending suit at the rate of £   .

The Applicant having applied in his/her petition (answer) for a Periodical Payments Order for himself/ herself has requested the Court to make such an Order at the same rate as above.

Signed (District Judge)   Dated

What to do if you object to this Order being made.

If you object to the making of such a Periodical Payments Order, you must notify the District Judge and the Applicant/Respondent of your objections within 14 days of this notice being served on you. If you do not do so, the District Judge may make an Order without notifying you further.

The court office at

is open between 10 am and 4 pm (4.30pm at the Principal Registry of the Family Division) Monday to Friday. When corresponding with the court, please address forms or letters to the Court Manager and quote the case number. If you do not do so, your correspondence may be returned.

Form I Notice of Request for Periodical Payments Order at same rate as Order for Maintenance Pending Suit

APPENDIX B
New Ancillary Relief Procedure
Note: the overriding objective in Rule 2.51B governs all steps

Phase 1: To end of First Appointment ('FA')

	Step	Party	Timing	FPR
1	Filing of Ancillary Relief Notice (Form A)	Either	Any time after filing Petition	2.61A(1)
2	Fixing of First Appointment **12-16 weeks** ahead (**Form C**) NB: No vacating of date without permission	Court	When Form A is filed	2.61A(4)(a) 2.61A(5)
3	Service of copy of Notice in Form A	Court	Within **4 days** after Form A filed	2.61A(4)(b)
4	Filing and **simultaneous exchange** of **Form E**, completed and sworn by each party and containing the information and attaching the documents **required** by the Form and any other documents **necessary** to explain or clarify the information. The **required** documents are • property valuations obtained in last 6 months • most recent mortgage statements • last 12 months' bank statements • surrender value quotes of insurance policies • last 2 years' business accounts • valuation of pension rights • last 3 payslips and most recent p60	Both	At least 35 **days** before FA	2.61B(1),(2)
5	Service of documents required by but unavoidably not attached to Form E (with explanation); but otherwise	Either	At earliest opportunity	2.61B(5)
	NO general discovery before FA	Neither		2.61B(6)
6	Filing and service of		At least **14 days** before FA	2.61(B)(7)
	• Concise statement of issues;	Both		
	• Chronology;	Both		
	• Questionnaire, **referable to the statement of issues**, seeking further information and documents; and	Both		
	• Notice (**Form G**) stating whether that party will be able to proceed to FDR at the FA	Both		
	and confirmation of service under FPR 2.59(3) & (4), and applicable 2.70(4)	Applicant		

	Step	Party	Timing	FPR
7	Produce first costs estimate (Form H)	Both	Immediately prior to FA	2.61F(1)
	If a party intends to seek a summary assessment of costs, produce a Woolf costs schedule		24 hours prior to FA	2.61F(2)
8	**THE FIRST APPOINTMENT**			
	Objective: to define issues and save costs	Both parties to attend personally unless otherwise ordered FPR 2.61D(5)	On date fixed 12-16 weeks after filing of Form A (Step 2)	2.61D(1)
	Directions as to:			
	• answering questions and producing documents; and any further **necessary** documentation;			2.61D(2)(a)
	• valuations (joint where appropriate) and experts			2.61D(2)(b)
	• evidence to be adduced by each party, further chronologies, schedules			2.61D(2)(b)
	District Judge *shall* then:			
	either direct FDR (this will be the norm)		Date for FDR on Form D	2.61D(2)(c)
	Or (if FDR in appropriate) direct:			2.61D(2)(d)
	• hearing for further directions; or			
	• hearing for interim order; or			
	• final hearing; or			
	• adjournment for mediation, negotiation or generally.			
	The District Judge *may* in addition			2.61D(2)(f)
	• make urgent interim order, provided application duly made in accordance with 2.69F returnable on that occasion;			
	• having regard to forms g (see step 6), treat as FDR			
	• direct pensions valuation			
	Costs			
	• produce written estimate to DJ	Both		2.61F
	• DJ must consider making an order for costs depending on circumstances including compliance with the rules.			2.61D(2)(e)

Phase 2: to end of Financial Dispute Resolution Appointment ('FDR')

	Step	Party	Timing	FPR
9	Comply with all directions made at FA	Both	As per Direction Order and by FDR date	
	Any further discovery only with court permission	Both	By application	2.61D(3)
10	Where FDR has been ordered:			
	Notice to court of all offers, proposals and responses, including all without prejudice and Calderbank offers	Applicant	At least **7 days** before	2.61E(3) 2.69 FDR
	Produce second costs estimate in Form H	Both	Immediately prior to FDR	2.61F
11	**THE FDR APPOINTMENT**			
	Objective: best endeavours to reach agreement	Both parties to attend personally unless otherwise ordered: FPR	On date fixed at FA	2.61E 2.61E(6)
	Ground rules:		2.61E(9)	
	• FDR treated as held for discussion and negotiation purposes: see Practice Direction [1997] 3 All ER 768, [1997] 1 WLR 1069			2.61E(1)
	• Conducted by a DJ who will not have anything else to do with the case			2.61E(2)
	• Offer details lodged are not to be kept on Court file after FDR			2.61E(5)
	District Judge may then:			
	• adjourn from time to time;			2.61E(7)
	• make appropriate consent order;			2.61E(8)
	• give further directions; and			
	• fix final hearing			
	Note: Where FDR has failed in a substantial case narrative affidavits of the financial history may be helpful: *W v W* (Wilson J, 17 January 2000, unreported)			
12	**Application for interim order**			
	• An application for an interim maintenance or variation order must be made returnable on 14 days notice	Either	At any time	2.69(F)
	• Unless the applicant has filed Form E it must be accompanied by a short sworn statement about his means and why the application is necessary			

Step	Party	Timing	FPR
• The other party must file and serve a short sworn statement of means not less than 7 days before the hearing • A party may at any stage apply (without notice if necessary) for other interim orders	Either	At any time	2.69(F)

Phase 3: to final hearing

	Step	Party	Timing	FPR
13	**Directions orders made at FDR to be complied with appropriately**	Both Order	As per Direction	
14	**Statement of Open Proposals** • To be drafted • File with Court and serve on other party	Both Applicant Respondent	After FDR **14 days** before final hearing **7 days after** receipt of Applicant's statement	2.69E(1) 2.69E(2)
15	**Further Directions/adjourned FDRs** A written statement of costs in Form H must be produced at every Court hearing	Either party may apply or Court may direct	Any time	2.61D(4) 2.61F
16	**THE FINAL HEARING** NB: Final costs estimate in Form H required		On date fixed at First Appointment (Step 8) or at FDR (Step 11) or otherwise	
17	**Costs after judgment** • Either party may make a *Calderbank* offer • Where a party beats his opponent's *Calderbank* offer, Court **must**, unless it considers it unjust, order the offeror to pay the offeree's costs from 28 days after the offer was made			2.69(1) 2.69B

Step	Party	Timing	Rule
• Where a party beats both his opponent's offer *and* his own offer, the court **may**, if it is just, order that for that period he receive indemnity costs and/or interest thereon of up to 10% over base rate			2.69C
• Factors affecting the justice of making such orders include the terms of *Calderbank* offers; the stage when made; the information then available; conduct of the parties; and their means			2.69D

APPENDIX C

PRE-APPLICATION PROTOCOL

1 Introduction

1.1

1.1.1 Lord Woolf in his final Access to Justice Report of July 1996 recommended the development of pre-application protocols.

'to build on and increase the benefits of early but well informed settlement which genuinely satisfy both parties to dispute'

1.1.2 In April 2000 the Lord Chancellor's Ancillary Relief Advisory Committee recommended that there be a Protocol for ancillary relief applications and this recommendation has been accepted by the Lord Chancellor.

1.2 The aim of the pre-application protocol is to ensure that:
(a) Pre-application disclosure and negotiation takes place in appropriate cases.
(b) Where there is pre-application disclosure and negotiation, it is dealt with
  (i) Cost effectively;
  (ii) In line with the overriding objectives of the Family Proceedings (Amendments) Rules 1999;
(c) The parties are in a position to settle the case fairly and early without litigation.

1.3 The court will be able to treat the standard set in the pre-application protocol as the normal reasonable approach to pre-application conduct. If proceedings are subsequently issued, the court will be entitled to decide whether there has been non-compliance with the protocol and, if so, whether non-compliance merits consequences.

2 Notes of Guidance

Scope of the Protocol

2.1 This protocol is intended to apply to all claims for ancillary relief as defined by FPR r 1(2). It is designed to cover all classes of case, ranging from a simple application for periodical payments to an application for a substantial lump sum and property adjustment order. The protocol is designed to facilitate the operation of what was called the pilot scheme and is from 5 June 2000 the standard procedure for ancillary relief applications

2.2 In considering the option of pre-application disclosure and negotiation, solicitors should bear in mind the advantage of having a court timetable and court managed process. There is sometimes an advantage in preparing disclosure before proceedings are commenced. However solicitors should bear in mind the objective of controlling costs and in particular the costs of discovery and that the option of pre-application disclosure and negotiation has risks of excessive and uncontrolled expenditure and delay. This option should only be encouraged where both parties agree to follow this route and disclosure is not likely to be an issue or has been adequately dealt with in mediation or otherwise.

2.3 Solicitors should consider at an early stage and keep under review whether it would be appropriate to suggest mediation to the clients as an alternative to solicitor negotiation or court based litigation.

2.4 Making an application to the court should not be regarded as a hostile step or a last resort, rather as a way of starting the court timetable, controlling disclosure and endeavouring to avoid the costly final hearing and the preparation for it.

First Letter

2.5 The circumstances of parties to an application for ancillary relief are so various that it would be difficult to prepare a specimen first letter. The request for information will be different in every case. However, the tone of the initial letter is important and the guidelines in para 3.7 should be followed. It should be approved in advance by the client. Solicitors writing to an unrepresented party should always recommend that he seeks independent legal advice and enclose a second copy of the letter to be passed to any solicitor instructed. A reasonable time limit for a response may be 14 days.

Negotiation and Settlement

2.6 In the event of pre-application disclosure and negotiation, as envisaged in paragraph 2.2 an application should not be issued when a settlement is a reasonable prospect.

Disclosure

2.7 The protocol underlines the obligation of parties to make full and frank disclosure of all material facts, documents and other information relevant to the issues. Solicitors owe their clients a duty to tell them in clear terms of this duty and of the possible consequences of breach of the duty. This duty of disclosure is an ongoing obligation and includes the duty to disclose any material changes after initial disclosure has been given. Solicitors are referred to the Good Practice Guide for Disclosure produced by the Solicitors Family Law Association (obtainable from the Administrative Director, 366A Crofton Road, Orpington, Kent BR2 8NN).

3.   The Protocol

General Principles

3.1 All parties must always bear in mind the overriding objective set out at FPR Rule 2.51B and try to ensure that all claims should be resolved and a just outcome achieved as speedily as possible without costs being unreasonably incurred. The needs of any children should be addressed and safeguarded. The procedures which it is appropriate to follow should be conducted with minimum distress to the parties and in a manner designed to promote as good a continuing relationship between the parties and any children affected as is possible in the circumstances.

3.2 The principle of proportionality must be borne in mind at all times. It is unacceptable for the costs of any case to be disproportionate to the financial value of the subject matter of the dispute.

3.3 Parties should be informed that where a court exercises a discretion as to whether costs are payable by one party to another, this discretion extends to pre-application offers to settle and conduct of disclosure. (Rule 44.3 Paragraph 1 of the Civil Procedure Rules 1998).

Identifying the Issues

3.4 Parties must seek to clarify their claims and identify the issues between them as soon as possible. So that this can be achieved, they must provide full, frank and clear disclosure of facts, information and documents which are material and sufficiently accurate to enable proper negotiations to take place to settle their differences. Openness in all dealings is essential.

Disclosure

3.5 If parties carry out voluntary disclosure before the issue of proceedings the parties should exchange schedules of assets, income, liabilities and other material facts, using Form E as a guide to the format of the disclosure. Documents should only be disclosed to the extent that they are required by Form E. Excessive or disproportionate costs should not be incurred.

Correspondence

3.6 Any first letter and subsequent correspondence must focus on the clarification of claims and identification of issues and their resolution. Protracted and unnecessary correspondence and 'trial by correspondence ' must be avoided.

3.7 The impact of any correspondence upon the reader and in particular the parties must always be considered. Any correspondence which raises irrelevant issues or which might cause the other party to adopt an entrenched, polarised or hostile position is to be discouraged.

Experts

3.8 Expert valuation evidence is only necessary where the parties cannot agree or do not know the value of some significant asset. The cost of a valuation should be proportionate to the sums in dispute. Wherever possible, valuations of properties, shares etc should be obtained from a single valuer instructed by both parties. To that end, a party wishing to instruct an expert (the first party) should first give the other party a list of the names of one or more experts in the relevant speciality whom he considers are suitable to instruct. Within 14 days the other party may indicate an objection to one or more of the named exerts and, if so, should supply the names of one or more experts whom he considers suitable.

3.9 Where the identity of the expert is agreed, the parties should agree the terms of a joint letter of instructions.

3.10   Where no agreement is reached as to the identity of the expert, each party should think carefully before instructing his own expert because of the costs implications. Disagreements about disclosure such as the use and identity of an expert may be better managed by the court within the context of an application for ancillary relief.

3.11   Whether a joint report is commissioned or the parties have chosen to instruct separate experts, it is important that the expert is prepared to answer reasonable questions raised by either party.

3.12   When experts' reports are commissioned pre-application, it should be made clear to the expert that they may in due course be reporting to the court and that they should therefore consider themselves bound by the guidance as to expert witnesses in Part 39 of the Civil Procedure Rules 1998.

3.13   Where the parties propose to instruct a joint expert, there is a duty on both parties to disclose whether they have already consulted that expert about the assets in issue.

3.14   If the parties agree to instruct separate experts the parties should be encouraged to agree in advance that the reports will be disclosed.

Summary

3.15   The aim of all pre-application proceedings steps must be to assist the parties to resolve their differences speedily and fairly or at least narrow the issues and, should that not be possible, to assist the Court to do so.